Orphan's Asylum

Sue
Take time to smell
the flowers —

Nick Kricorian

Orphan's Asylum

Mike Krecioch

To order additional copies of this book, contact:
Xlibris Corporation
1-888-795-4274
www.Xlibris.com
Orders@Xlibris.com
41780

CONTENTS

DEDICATION

This is dedicated to all the Felician Sisters who served at St. Hedwig Orphanage. Theirs was not an easy task. These dedicated women were expected to be both father and mother to the thousands of children who were in their care.

Also included are all the "orphinks" who spent time at St. Hedwig Orphanage. Only they know the true meaning of a childhood lost.

Finally, I must include my wife Sandi. She has been my friend, partner, nagger, lover, proofreader, agent, and inspiration. She has been the driving force for the completion of this project. Thank you, thank you, thank you.

MY FATHER

I was in the market the other day when I ran into someone who had known my father for several years prior to his passing. This person proceeded to tell me what a wonderful man he had been and how good he was to the kids in the neighborhood. I could not help but feel a bit bewildered after hearing those comments. I knew a different man.

It started in 1984 when I went to visit my uncle Felix in Los Angeles. He told me about my father and how he retired in Florida in 1980. This was all news to me because my father and I had not spoken to each other for eight or nine years. He told me how my father had acclimated to his new home and how all the neighbors loved him. Uncle Felix loved Florida too. His plans were to move to Florida when he retired from his CPA business, but that was not to be. He was dying of cancer. He did ask me to patch things up with my dad. My relationship with my dad at that point was estranged, to say the least, but I promised my uncle that I would attempt reconciliation. I would have done anything for my uncle Felix.

I kept my word and visited my dad in Florida. It was a very nice visit. He would not let me buy a thing. He was always stuffing money into my pocket. After the week's visit was over, he gave me another $150 for "spending money." He was difficult to refuse. I had a lot to think about on the flight back to Los Angeles.

This was a changed man from the man I used to know. All the neighbors did love him like he was family. The children in the neighborhood had nothing but good things to say about him. He apparently always had time for them. Where was he when I needed him, when I was growing up?

When my dad passed away in 1995, five of my cousins from Chicago showed up for the funeral. I had not seen any of them for thirty-five to forty years. All five of them indicated what a wonderful man my father had been and how lucky I was that he had been my father. They all had stories to tell about the many visits my dad had made to their homes when they were growing up. This was during the time when my brother and sister and I were incarcerated in an orphanage on the north side of Chicago. I don't remember these cousins coming to visit us. Maybe some of them did.

I resented these cousins for the time they shared with my father. It was a time that should have been spent with me, my brother Raymond, and my sister Sandra.

Yes, I said orphanage. My father put us in an orphanage for over eight years. He never referred to it as an orphanage though. He called it "boarding school." Was that the guilt rearing its ugly head? Or was it ignorance? In his defense, though, he never did miss a Visiting Sunday.

I would like to recount those years. Relive them. Take a close look at those times. Was it all that bad? I think not. Is it the solution to today's domestic problems, specifically broken homes? Probably not. Join me as I go back in time to living in Chicago starting in 1945, just after the war. The names, characteristics, and situations of some of the individuals in this book have been changed to protect their identities.

LOSS

Living on the south side of Chicago in 1945 was okay, I guess. I had nothing to compare it to. I was about five years old when Bruce and I raided our icebox and stole a couple of eggs apiece. We walked over to the main drag, 120th Street and Union Avenue, and started hurling eggs at the windshields of the shiny cars driving by. It seemed to me that all the cars were black in color. At least that's the way I remember it. I connected with the windshield of a car but wasn't expecting what happened next. The guy driving the car slammed on the brakes, jumped out of the car, and started chasing Bruce and me. I was a quicker runner and made a beeline for home a half block away. Bruce was caught almost immediately. I was hiding under our front porch when I noticed the very irate motorist walking with Bruce in tow. He was holding Bruce by the upper arm with a very strong grip. I watched the man and Bruce ascend the many steps to the four-flat apartment building next door where Bruce lived with his mom and dad. His mom was nice, but I really liked his dad. He drove a Birely soft drink truck. He always remembered us kids in the neighborhood. But I am going off on a tangent. No one was home at Bruce's, which was par for the course. Just like no one was home at my place. I watched the two of them descend the steps at Bruce's and walk over to my house. The fuming man knocked on the door. In fact, he pounded on that door.

I yelled out, "No one is home," without thinking from my hiding place under the porch. All I heard was "Come here, you little shit!" I did not stick around to be introduced. I ran and jumped over a fence or two. I knew he couldn't keep up because he was being slowed down by Bruce. He would not let go of him. About an hour later, I saw Bruce in the alley. I yelled to him and asked if it was clear. He waved me over. I did not see the upset male motorist anywhere in the vicinity. We laughed about the situation. I thought for sure Bruce would be mad at me. Hell, I can't help it if I'm a better runner.

Surviving on the south side was a way of life if you know what you are doing. Neither of us would get in trouble on this day because the irate motorist had better things to do than hang around and wait for our folks to get home. He left a note in the mailbox on my porch, but I made sure that no one saw the note. Our family lived in a two-bedroom, four-flat apartment rental that was owned by my grandmother, my mom's mother. So anyone could have found that note. This five-year-old was learning to survive in the "big city." Both of my folks were working, and someone had to take care of me.

Memories of my mom are vague. I recall her and dad always bickering about something. She worked for the telephone company in downtown Chicago. He worked for the "hammer shop," American Brake Shoe, located at 119th Street and Halsted. It looked like a steel mill to me. As near as I could figure, when my dad was at work, Mom was supposed to be home. When Mom was at work, Dad was supposed to be at home. I think that was the way it was intended to work. I never could figure out or remember what specific shifts they worked. One of them did work some sort of split shift. This was rather confusing to this five-year-old mind. I may have been an exceptionally sharp kid, but I didn't profess to know it all. Those events occurred so many years ago.

Kindergarten and first grade at West Pullman Elementary School had fond memories for me. Across the street from the school was the neatest diner in the world. My dad had taken me there many times, especially when my mom was working. It was neat because my dad made arrangements with the owner for me to have my lunch in this establishment on school days. This I did on an almost-daily basis. I did not have to pay any money. My dad would take care of it at the end of each week. Well, he did not know that I was interested in the girls in my class. I would take the girls, one at a time, and have lunch with them at my own private diner. When my dad got the bill for the first week, he remarked that I sure did eat a lot. I wasn't about to tell him otherwise. I went through most of first grade before he got wind of what I was doing. I blew it by taking my buddies two or three at a time.

From that point on, I had to make my own lunch. Peanut butter and jelly sandwiches. Salami or baloney when it was available. My dad or my mom would get me up in the morning. They would get ready for work, and I would get ready for my long day at school, such as it was. They would tell me what time I had to leave the house in order to get to school on time. I guess I knew how to tell time. I don't remember what they did with my younger brother and sister, Raymond and Sandra. They were probably hauled off to the upstairs-neighbor lady.

One time I recall making toast for my younger siblings. The toaster was the old-fashioned, wired type, which sat right on top of the gas burner. I was playing around with a balloon when it got knocked into the toaster and broke. The smell was the foulest I had ever remembered in my young life. It scared the hell out of all three of us. There were no parents at home at that time. I wonder what the going rate for a five-year-old babysitter was back in 1945. But I made their toast and put a lot of peanut butter and jam on their slices. Even now, I find it hard to believe that I was taking care of them at the age of five or six. That would make them about two and three years old. Scary. The sad part is that I really thought I could handle any emergency that came up. My brother was always in diapers and covered from head to toe with dirt. My sister ventured out into the neighborhood on her own. Early on, she learned to take care of herself. She did not need me. She was one tough cookie. Her foul mouth put the fear of God into more than a couple of neighbors. I recall one incident when she got into trouble for chasing one of the neighborhood kids out of our yard and down the street. The kid was twice her size, but Sandra wielded a wicked broom. She also let fly a litany of her infamous cuss words. Where she picked up that kind of language was a mystery. Neither our mother nor father used that type of language.

I recall being instructed to knock on the upstairs-neighbor lady's door if "something came up," whatever that was supposed to be. In addition, if the neighbor lady was not available, I had been instructed to go to the corner tavern and notify the bartender. Apparently, the owner of the bar knew of our situation. In retrospect, I suppose that was comforting.

My parents split up in March 1947. One day they were together, and the next they weren't. Anybody could have seen it was inevitable. After all, both set of their parents were constantly butting into their affairs. My dad's parents treated my mom as an outcast because she was Hungarian. Better said, they did not accept her because she was not of Polish origin. Come to think of it, the Polish people in Chicago were and still are very clannish. They did stick together. Even now, in the old Polish neighborhoods, numerous Polish households refuse to sell their homes and move elsewhere. This was their way of life, despite the fact that the white flight occurred thirty years ago. I guess they were just plain stubborn.

It suddenly hit me that my mom was no longer around. She just wasn't part of my life anymore. I had many aunts and uncles, on my dad's side of the family, who were quick to take her place. They meant well, but I certainly resented it. I really liked my mom. All the aunts and uncles used to say bad things about her. They did not know what they were talking about. After all, I was present at some of the incidents, and I did not remember the event the way they told it. This is about the time in my life that I found out that you cannot trust everything that is told to you. I learned not to trust adults, especially adult relatives. Let's just say that I had to grow up in a hurry.

Shortly after my mom was gone, my dad and I lived together for about a month. An aunt and uncle took my brother and sister in for a while, probably for that whole month. I loved living with my dad for that short time. It was just the two of us, and I had hoped this special time with him would last forever. He let me do things that no parent in his/her right mind would allow. He would send me to the store to purchase new comic books. This was often done after ten o'clock at night. The store was about two blocks from the house. I knew which ones he liked, and he trusted my judgment. *Batman, Superman*, war stories, true crime, and detective stories. We both enjoyed reading the comics. Amazing. Was this the method used to teach me to read? He once told me to buy myself some ice cream, and I brought home a half gallon of vanilla. He let me eat the whole thing. That was a whole lot of ice cream. It was probably my supper for that evening.

Not having my brother and sister to watch over had been a real treat. Then, suddenly, they were there. Delivered by our aunt and uncle. The three of us were about to embark on another adventurous chapter in life.

AUNTS AND UNCLES

One day in May 1948, I found myself sitting in my dad's Chevy with my brother and sister. They seemed so little to me and angelic. But I knew better, especially in the case of my sister. Since she had the foulest mouth in the neighborhood, she taught me all the bad words I dared to use. There we were, sitting in the downtown area of Chicago, sitting for hours in a locked car. Little did I know, the divorce hearing was in full progress. And there I was, babysitting again. My dad sure trusted me. I don't know if I would have trusted myself like that. While I am sitting in his car, I saw my first black man. I could not believe it. My friends had told me that a black man's skin is really dark, but this man's skin was very, very dark. I wanted to open the door and get a closer look, but I remembered my dad telling me not to unlock the car doors. I was fascinated with this man. He was probably in his forties, gaunt looking and wearing raggedy clothing. I remember that as he walked, he was devouring a pound cake. The way he was eating the cake led me to believe that he was really hungry. His shoes were very worn, about to fall off his feet. My seven-year-old mind informed me that I was probably looking at my first "homeless" person. I did wonder where he lived.

After several days, we all moved out of our rental and in with my aunt and uncle. Aunt Veronica was a character. She always seemed to be cooking something in the kitchen. She was a hefty woman, strong and demanding. She had a son the same approximate age as me. He had been an only child. We were probably good company for each other. Too bad it had to end when it did. It may have made a better person out of him, but to put it bluntly, he was a spoiled jerk. My cousin Bill could do no wrong. When the two of us would screw up, I was the one who got punished. The punishments were a bit on the weird side. My aunt would make me sleep on the wooden floor under the bed we shared. I was to stay under the bed until my dad got home from work. That was usually about midnight. Then I was allowed out to tell him my side of the story.

My dad always looked tired and never gave his sister any argument. In fact, he never went to bat for me. At least I knew exactly where I stood. Once again, I had to look out for myself. My aunt seemed to hate me. I liked my uncle, but he was never around. Uncle Fred was a short, chubby guy, always chewing on something. And he was funny. He seemed to have a flatulence problem on which he capitalized. He kept us kids laughing.

Somehow, I knew my dad was caught in a situation where he did not have much in the way of options. I just played it cool while I lived there. Forty years later, I found out that my dad damn near had a nervous breakdown. He was seeing a therapist weekly for the longest time. Those were not fun days.

I even went to Catholic school with my cousin Bill. They placed me in the second grade. I seemed to be behind all the other kids as far as writing was concerned. I was still printing while the rest of the class was already engaged in cursive writing. I was able to dazzle my teacher with my reading ability. I even learned to read, write, and properly pronounce the Polish words. I had no idea what they meant, but the pronunciation was good.

My younger cousin, who was in the first grade, always seemed to be getting into trouble with the older boys in this school. Guess who had to come to his defense time and time again? Of course, I was kept after school by the nuns for fighting. Some of these guys were big, but I was stupid enough to take them on. I held my own though. My aunt Veronica, uncle Fred, and cousin Bill have always thought very highly of me for fighting his battles. I personally didn't think I was very bright in those days.

Since it wasn't working out with my aunt and uncles, they shipped me out to stay with my dad's parents, my grandma and grandpa. They lived about six blocks away. I liked it there. The whole house was my domain. My three uncles and two aunts were still living at home. Let's just say that there was always someone to talk to. It was a big house, and I was well cared for. My brother and sister didn't come along, so I assumed they stayed at my aunt and uncle's house.

One of my uncles was gay and eventually became a heroin addict. He was a World War II vet and had seen his share of action. He spent hours with me, showing me the photographs of the battleships firing their barrages at the islands in the Pacific during the war. He was one of the nicer uncles. It's a small wonder that he is still very much alive today. This man has led one horrendous life. I even liked his "friend." They were both very good to me.

My aunts and uncles did not talk down to me like some relatives do. My aunt Becky, my dad's youngest sister, treated me pretty well. She used to share me with her girlfriends, teenagers like herself. Her friends would make a fuss over my hair and my long eyelashes. You talk about a kid in seventh heaven; here are all these gorgeous teen queens giving me hugs and pecks on the cheek. Of course, I ate it up. I even got to take a motorcycle ride with her boyfriend. My aunt Becky was the beauty queen of the family. It's a shame she died at the age of forty. Leukemia, just like one of my uncles. Leukemia must have run in the family.

My grandpa was good to me. He was a tall, powerful man. You could tell he worked hard most of his life. He had muscles on his muscles. My grandma was so sweet. She wasn't exactly little, but she did move gracefully. Sometimes I had a hard time understanding the two of them because they spoke very little English. Usually only Polish was spoken in this household. One of my uncles or aunts was always around to translate. It was even more fun than living with my dad alone. I ate pretty well too. A lot of *kielbasa* (polish sausage), *kluski* (noodles), *kapusta* (cabbage), *pierogi* (stuffed dumpling), *kasia* (blood and rice sausage), carrots, and potatoes. I always sprinkled a lot of sugar on my tomatoes. The beans and peas were always fresh from the garden. I did a lot of the weeding in the garden to help pay for my keep.

I certainly enjoyed myself at my grandparents. This was one of the happiest times of my childhood. The biggest reason was the absence of Raymond and Sandra. There were no little ones to look after. Is this a terrible thing to say? Not if you were the one having to keep an eye on them. At the age of seven, I must have experienced what we now call stress. Isn't that incredible?

I only spent about two or three months at my grandparents' house. The clue that things were coming to an end occurred when my dad mentioned something about a "boarding school." I did not comprehend where this was going. If I paid more attention, the shock would not have been so great. In October 1948, my dad drove his brand-new Chevrolet over to my grandparents' house. I ran out to the curb to greet him and discovered that he had my brother and sister with him. I had not seen my brother or sister for what seemed like months. The next thing I know, my uncle Felix, my all-time favorite relative, is carrying two shopping bags to the car. I did not realize that all my possessions were in those two bags. I was a perceptive little kid and knew immediately that we were all going on a trip. I was not experiencing happy thoughts about the travel arrangements. My dad was unusually talkative when he invited me to sit up front with him. It seemed that he was giving me a history lesson of all the places the four of us had been living for the past couple of years. I knew what he was getting at, but I did not fully understand the finality of the arrangements he had made. This happy family was "boarding school" bound, like it or not. It was clear over on the north side of Chicago, away from all family members. That was almost like going to another country. Why?

THE ARRIVAL

On a clear, cool October day in 1948, my dad drove his Chevy into a gated driveway just off the main highway located at Harlem and Touhy Avenue. It was considered out in the sticks in those days. The grounds of the "boarding school" went on forever and ever, sprawled over forty-two acres. He finally turned down a very long circular driveway to a three-story redbrick building. A short, unusually dressed woman, who I found out later was a nun, came out of the building to greet us. Her name was Sister Teresita. She was wearing a black and brown nun's habit. Her head was completely covered with a helmetlike device made of starched linen. It hid her head and hair. All you could see was her rounded face. The ears were not visible. She wore glasses and a ready smile. She was the first of many nuns I would meet during the next few weeks. And they all dressed the same way. Sister Teresita was nice enough, but there was something about the situation that disturbed me. Then I saw her, Valerie Dingster. Valerie Dingster was introduced to us, and it became evident that we would be dealing with her quite a bit during the next week.

Valerie was Sister Teresita's helper. Sister Teresita was the resident nurse of St. Hedwig Orphanage and Industrial School. She was going to inspect us for lice and any possible communicable diseases. We were going to be quarantined for a full week. She was talking with my dad while Valerie showed us the playroom. My brother and sister immediately went for the broken toys, which were strewn about the brightly lit room. The sun shone through the windows, warming the room. It resembled someone's screened back porch, only this was within the building at the end of the corridor. Raymond and Sandra appeared comfortable. I stood "guard," watching Valerie staring at my little brother and sister. Valerie was probably about thirty-five years old but looked much older. She didn't talk like a normal woman. It sounded more like a cackle. She wasn't the most pleasant-looking person. Her hair was scraggly and somewhat sparse. I had never seen a balding woman, not ever, until now.

She muttered a lot, Valerie did. My name immediately became "Hey, you." She did not appear to be in full control of her faculties. She scared me.

When I looked around for my father, I noticed he had somehow gotten into his car unobserved. He started to drive away. I was sure the good sister and Valerie kept us kids busy so that he could make his getaway. I ran outside to where the car had been parked and yelled for my dad to stop. I could see him accelerating the vehicle about fifty feet away from me. Whether he saw me in his rearview mirror or not, I will never know. He did not appear to look back.

Sandra and Raymond are at my side asking where Daddy is going. I have to explain to these two little tykes that Daddy is going to his home and that this place is now our home. Both of them were in tears as I spoke to them. Now the flood really started. There was nothing I could do to stop them from crying. That moment is one of those that are etched in my memory for all time. If I had known then that I was to spend the next eight plus years of my life in that school, I don't think I would have tried to make the best of a bad situation. At that point, I did not even know when I would see my dad again. I had a whole bunch of questions for him. I wanted and needed some answers so I could deal with Raymond and Sandra. Looking back at that moment in my life, the anger within me was at the height of intensity. To this day, I have never, ever been more upset.

The three of us walked back into the building, and I directed them to the playroom. They were crying their little hearts out. If I didn't have them to look after (here we go again), I would have been crying myself. I knew I couldn't cry on that occasion, and that was probably the last time I have ever even considered doing it for a long, long time, well into my adult years. How does a seven-year-old kid suppress his emotions without causing some sort of short circuit later on in life? God only knows. Somebody must have been looking out for me though.

I don't know how I did it, but hours later I was able to calm Raymond and Sandra. Suddenly, it was dinnertime. Another nun had prepared the meal (thank God, it wasn't Valerie Dingster) and had kept checking on us kids. She seemed to feel sympathy for us, but she uttered nary a word. Valerie entered our dining area, muttering to herself, then to us, to hurry up so she could clean up. Valerie frequently spoke to herself quite clearly. The woman was full of constant conversation. Valerie was a very scary person.

Raymond and Sandra had difficulty eating anything. I did not feel like eating either. I managed to eat part of my portion, but I had to sneak the food off our plates and toss it. Who knows what these people would do to us for wasting food. I managed and took the dishes into a kitchen area just off the dining room. Raymond and Sandra went into the playroom and attempted to amuse themselves.

I went exploring. I wanted to figure out what this building was and what it was used for. It almost felt like a hospital. I went down the long corridor and noted that most of the doors were closed. I tried to open several, but they were locked. One that I did open looked like a waiting room in a doctor's or dentist's office. Then I tried the inside door to what would have been the doctor's office, "Bingo!" The first room was a doctor's examining room. The room next to it was obviously a dentist's torture chamber including a fully equipped dental chair. I vacated the premises quickly. The two rooms gave me the creeps. I came to a staircase and climbed to the second floor. Continuing down the hall, I found three wardrooms with four beds in each room. Several more wardrooms contained eight or ten beds per room. The place was looking more and more like a hospital. I found out later that it was referred to as an infirmary. The reason we were being kept there was a mystery to me. If this is a boarding school, where are the other kids? All I have seen so far are two nuns and Valerie Dingster.

My worst fears were realized when Valerie caught me looking in the rooms upstairs. She cackled at me and directed me down to the playroom. Of course, there was nothing in the playroom to amuse me. There were some books, but half the pages were ripped out. Valerie came into the room at about 8:00 p.m. and told us to put the toys away. It was bedtime. She led the three of us up the stairs. I had my own wardroom just off the main corridor. The kids were at least kept together in what appeared to be a nursery room with cribs. It was nicely painted with goofy pictures and murals on the walls. The whole infirmary was spotless. I did not find a speck of dust anywhere. The floors shined brightly. I asked Valerie who kept the place so clean. She told me that she did. The way she answered me, I was not going to dispute her statement.

Sandra and Raymond were sobbing while they were getting dressed for bed. All our clothing magically appeared in a closet within the room. The clothing must have been sneaked into the building when I was preoccupied with Valerie. God, that woman scared me.

The sobs of Sandra and Raymond were quieting down. They were probably two rooms away from me, and I could hear their little whimpers. I hoped they would be able to get a good night's sleep. I was concerned whether or not I would. I wondered why my brother and sister could not share one of the wardrooms. This was traumatic for all three of us. But I did not dare ask.

As I laid down on the hospital-type bed, I looked up at the ceiling and attempted to piece together the events of the past day. Things were happening too fast. I just could not keep track. My head was spinning, and before you knew it, I must have fallen deep asleep.

A bright, sunny day greeted me the next morning. The room was exceptionally bright from the sunlight. The sun shone right into my face. The windows had roll-up shades, which apparently were never used. I got up to lower the shade, and the whole thing came crashing down. Valerie came into the room, muttering to herself, muttering something about kids getting worse and worse. I swear to God she was a nut case who escaped from an institution. Come to think of it, the school of which the infirmary was a part of was referred to as an "institution." That also concerned me. That really made me wonder about the place we were in and how Valerie Dingster fit into the program. I distinctly got the impression that I should be more concerned than I was.

Is it possible that my dad had delivered us to a mental hospital? I figured that I would be better off if I kept my thoughts to myself, at least for the time being. Don't say anything to Raymond and Sandra. They probably would not comprehend what was going on anyway. Valerie picked up the window shade and told me to get dressed. She informed me that Sandra and Raymond were downstairs eating their breakfast already and that I had better get it in gear. No way was I going to argue with her. No way.

I got downstairs and walked into the dining room. There sat my brother and sister, eating farina, with a disoriented look on their faces. The poor things had no idea what was going on. Sister Teresita came into the room and told me to take Sandra and Raymond for a walk after we finished our breakfast. She warned me not to leave the circular driveway. I acknowledged her request and finished eating. After I picked up all our dishes and carried them into the kitchen area, the second nun told me to leave them in the sink. Oh well, I was perfectly capable of cleaning our dishes, but I did not want to make waves. Not just yet.

After putting their jackets on, I took Sandra and Raymond for a walk around the long circular driveway. It was rather chilly out. However, the October air was refreshing. The privet bushes were neatly trimmed, standing about three feet tall. It looked like someone gave them a flattop haircut. As we got about fifty feet from the infirmary building, I noticed a cavelike area. Upon investigating it, I noted that it was a grotto with a life-sized statue of Jesus. At the base of the statue was a fishpond just loaded with goldfish. Tiny, little ones. I wondered what they did with the goldfish during the winter when everything was frozen over. We continued walking to the end of the driveway near the entrance where my dad had driven into the premises. That's when I noted the large four-story redbrick building. The building went on forever and ever. It seemed to be one full block long. At the center of the building was an extension, which jutted out probably two hundred feet. I found out later that this was the chapel. The stained glass windows were a clue. I wanted to go check things out, but I was stuck with my brother and sister again. Babysitting. When will it end?

We were incarcerated in the infirmary for one whole week. Quarantined. The doctor and the dentist gave us a real going-over. All three of us were pronounced in perfect health. However, the dentist examined my mouth and could not believe what he saw. Huge cavities, numerous. To put it in his words, "I never saw such deep cavities. You have the capability to grow potatoes in your cavities." I'm sure he meant to be funny, but we did not hit it off at all. I did not like him. I found out really quick how much he did not like me when he filled one of my teeth without benefit of enough Novocain. That was the one incident that turned me against dentists for a long, long time. His name was Dr. Wroblewski. He was a bit chunky, not fat, and wore glasses with metal rims. Probably about thirty-five years old. He drove a white-and-pink Cadillac. As an adult, I've had dreams about that pink car of his.

The story was that this dentist had been raised at St. Hedwig Orphanage years ago, and the monsignor footed the bill for him when he was sent to college. In fact, the monsignor also footed the bill for medical school. Now every other Wednesday was his day to pay back the monsignor by taking care of the kids at the orphanage. I've since been told that he had antiquated equipment and did the best that he could under the circumstances. It was probably very noble of him to try to pay back the monsignor, but I don't think I will ever forget him. I thought that he was a mediocre dentist who had a big bill to pay. Most of the kids ended up fearing and hating him. I did all I could to avoid him. Suffice it to say, I never looked forward to his visits. However, avoidance was not always an option.

PURGATORY

This was the big day. The day that Raymond, Sandra, and I were going to be introduced to the mainstream orphanage folk. I don't know what happened to my brother and sister. All of a sudden, they had been led away by a nun I had never seen before. I did not see them until that afternoon for lunch. I wondered what my new teacher would be like. Or my dormitory nun. I had been told that I would be placed in the third grade. I would have a teaching sister and a dormitory sister. Here, it was the middle of October, and I was finally going to attend school. I was looking forward to school. I actually missed it.

I thought I would never be able to tell these nuns apart—they all dressed alike—but I was doing a pretty good job at it. Some were taller than others, some wider. Some even appeared friendly while others did not.

I was escorted into the main office of St. Hedwig Orphanage by Sister Teresita. The nun behind the counter asked me some questions, which I don't remember. She then dismissed Sister Teresita and told me to follow her to my class. If I recall correctly, the classroom was located on the first floor of the main building several doors down from the main office. This building had three floors. The dormitories were located on the upper floors. To the best of my recollection, the top floor was for the older kids—high school as well as seventh and eighth grades. The dormitories on the second floor were for grades 3 through 6. The youngest, those in kindergarten and first and second grades, had a separate dormitory on the main (first) floor of the building, the same floor as the classrooms and the library.

My introduction to my third-grade teacher was made by the office nun. She introduced my teacher as Sister Mary Hilarion, three distinct and separate names. I found out later that all nuns' names were preceded by Sister Mary. The office nun gave Sister Hilarion some paperwork of mine and then left. I felt like a lamb being led to slaughter. Sister Hilarion smiled at me and stated, "Class, this is Michael." I immediately retaliated, "No, it's Mike." I guess I came across as one who had a chip on the shoulder. It was not intentional, but I was not about to let these new kids call me by a name that only a select few would ever call me. I continued this attitude throughout my life. To this day, I can count on one hand the number of people, relatives included, who call me Michael.

Sister Hilarion motioned for me to take a vacant seat toward the rear of the room. I looked over the gathering of boys and girls and noted that there were twenty-two students, fourteen boys and eight girls. I started walking toward the rear of the classroom when halfway down the aisle, one of the bigger boys stuck his foot out to trip me. I saw it coming and gave his ankle a hard kick. I wasn't about to take crap from anyone, especially some orphan kid. He yelped out loud, and Sister Hilarion demanded to know what happened. I quickly answered that I had tripped on his big foot. This caused laughter in the class, and it also made the owner of the offending foot laugh. Starting out on the "wrong foot" suddenly became the "right foot" for me. Several of the boys grinned at me, nodding their approval of what I had done to Mr. Troublemaker's foot. All the girls smiled at me. I suppose that in my own way, I put everyone on notice that I was not a pushover. I was going to defend myself. Defend? Actually, I learned a long time ago that the best defense is a good offense, long before football made that a popular phrase. If someone was going to give me some trouble, make 'em pay right up front. Pounce on 'em. Remember, I am a survivor of the south side of Chicago. Stay out of my way.

I liked Sister Hilarion. She came across like a disciplinarian, but she did have a softer side. That first day in class, she read a story out of a book, stopped, looked at me, and said, "Would Mike like to read for the class?" I quickly responded, "Yes, ma'am." Everyone in the class cringed. I could just feel it. But why? I guess they were not accustomed to a nun being referred to as "ma'am." I learned very quickly that a nun was referred to as "Sister," nothing else. She motioned me up to the front of the room, handed me the book, pointed to where she wanted me to start, and then I started reading. After several minutes of reading, flawlessly I might add, Sister Hilarion motioned me to stop. She asked me where I learned to read so well. I don't recall if I ever gave her an answer. Reading is something I have always been able to do. I was only eight years old, but I could read most adult books. And the adult words I was not familiar with, well, I just consulted Mr. Dictionary. To this day, I could not tell you who or how I managed to learn to read. Let's just say that Sister Hilarion and I hit it off. I may not have made many points with my classmates, but such was life. The survivor in me was hitting third gear. Prior to my arrival at St. Hedwig, my only contact with nuns was at my previous school, BVM, on the south side of Chicago. Those nuns were too busy disciplining me to notice whether or not I had any talent.

Being the "new kid" at St. Hedwig had its advantages. The new kid wasn't supposed to know what the drill was, what one could get away with, etc. Ha! I was one up on them. It did not take me long to figure out who was a threat and who could be trusted. I quickly learned that if you participated in Sister Hilarion's class, involved yourself in discussions, asked reasonable questions, Sister Hilarion was going to be your buddy. Let's just say that for the entire third grade, Sister Hilarion cut me a lot of slack. I took it upon myself to change her opinion of me in the last week of the semester. It was probably early June 1949. I had been fighting a cold off and on all spring. After a particularly noisy bout of coughing, Sister Hilarion commanded me to partake of the cough medicine. Each classroom had a quart of cough medicine, red in color, which probably had a very high content of alcohol. I walked to the front of the classroom and, instead of using the spoon provided, removed the cap from the cough medicine, lifted the bottle to my lips, and chugalugged more than an ounce or two of the medicine. I walked back to my seat, sat down, and decided that I liked the taste of the cough medicine. During the break, when everyone else left the room to use the bathrooms, I lagged behind and took another taste of the medicine.

When we resumed class about ten minutes later, I brazenly walked up to the medicine bottle, picked it up, and placed it to my lips.

"What do you think you are doing?" barked Sister Hilarion. I never broke stride. I continued to partake of the cough medicine and down went another several ounces. By this time, I was feeling the effects of some rather potent cough medicine. I must say that I was probably bombed out of my mind. I recalled talking a lot, and fast. Sister Hilarion finally figured out what I had done, and I was on her "list" for the remainder of the school year.

She must not have held it against me too seriously because I was named "Student of the Year." Even though I had the highest grade point average in the class, the teacher always had the option of making the final decision. Maybe she saw the humor in what had happened. I have always thought that Sister Hilarion was one of the more humanistic contacts in my near decade at St. Hedwig.

LIFE OF AN "INMATE"

I recall that my first month in the mainstream of the orphanage was a real eye-opener. Everything was done in formation, two by two. Everywhere you went. First- and second-graders were required to hold hands. They tried to make the third- and fourth-graders hold hands, but there was too much resistance. The nuns finally let it go. But that was the only thing they let pass.

Six-thirty in the morning was the normal wake-up call for all grades. The bustle of activity could be felt, if not heard, throughout the building. We were roused from our cots by Sister Felicia with the obnoxiously loud clapping of her hands. What a rude awakening. All my newly found buddies seemed to know what to do. Everyone grabbed their toothbrushes and toothpastes and marched to the large bathroom just around the corner of the dormitory. At this point in my life, I did not know what a toothbrush was or what it was used for. I had never owned one. But I followed the crowd anyway. We were all in our underwear bottoms, some in jockeys and some in boxers. Everyone washed their face at the two rows of sinks located in the middle of the large room. The older kids were required to use the two rows of sinks on the walls. All forty sinks were being used. The hot water was plenty hot. I waited for the first available sink and then rinsed my face with cold water. It was a real eye-opener. After drying my face, I made a beeline for the dorm. Everyone seemed to be in a hurry. I was no exception. We dressed and made up our beds. Of course, my bed was not made up properly and my potential buddies let me know it. One even told Sister Felicia that the "new kid" didn't make up his bed "the way he is supposed to." Sister Felicia, wise in the ways of child rearing, responded, "Then you teach him to make it properly." He did.

Sister Felicia clapped her hands, and all the boys filed out of the dorm into the hallway, lined up in column of twos. It may not have been done in strict military fashion, but it was close. We walked toward the center of the building to a staircase, down the staircase to the second floor, then continued walking in column of twos toward the chapel. Chapel? I thought chapels were supposed to be small churches. This place was huge. I had never been in a church this large. Sister Felicia led us into church to a particular pew and had us single file ourselves in place. I looked around and noted that other nuns were doing the same with their charges. It appeared that I was going to be sitting in practically the same place every time I came to the chapel.

Each grade had their own assigned row or rows of seats. Off to my left was the girls' side of the church. All the girls were filing in single file by grade. My first observation was that there were almost twice as many boys as there were girls. A lot of the girls were older, that is, preteens and teenagers.

Mass was performed by Fr. Francis S. Rusch, the headmaster of the facility. He performed the Mass in approximately twenty-two minutes. Little did I know it at the time, but the monsignor was known for his quick masses. When Mass was over and before the monsignor even left the sanctuary, the older kids, toward the rear of the church, were filing out to go to breakfast. It took no time at all to empty the church. All hands were headed to the main dining room. Being a Monday, it was probably a cornflakes day or whatever, if cereal happened to be in good supply. Usually everyone got the same. No exceptions. However, not only was there cornflakes in each bowl at each place setting, there was also a metal pitcher of diluted coffee on each table. The coffee was quite good, diluted with milk and seasoned with plenty of sugar. I did not know young guys like me could have coffee at my tender age of eight. I loved it.

After eating, one was required to carry his or her bowl, cup, and spoon to the front of the dining room. There were two windowlike openings to what I learned was the *kanapka*. The Kanapka was the room that housed the large dishwasher. All the dishes were brought to the large window opening. The attendants were all older boys, probably sixth grade or higher. They sure kept busy handling all the dishes and utensils. They placed the dishes on wire-type trays, loaded the tray into the dishwasher, and hit a button, which in turn activated the machine. Hot, soapy water inundated the dishes from nozzles atop and below the opening. Somehow, there was a rinse cycle, but with exceptionally hot water. In the years to come, I would become quite adept at handling the dishwasher, hot water and all.

On the way out of the dining room area, I was reminded by one of the nuns to "hurry, hurry, hurry." I made my way back to the dormitory on the third floor and noted that there was much activity. Apparently after breakfast, all boys had their assigned chores. I was the new kid and did not have an assignment yet. This was the week for the third grade to clean the bathroom. And clean it they did. Some of the boys used long-handled brushes and were scrubbing the toilets with scouring powder. Others were scouring the sinks with clean rags. Two of the boys were waiting for everyone to finish up so that they could scrub and mop the floor. Everyone was in a hurry. Come to think of it, even when we were eating our breakfast, there was a nun going from table to table reminding everyone to hurry. "Don't spend all your time talking. Eat your food and get out of here. You have chores to do before class."

By 8:30 a.m., we were seated at our desks in the classroom, boys on one side and girls on the other. I wasn't so sure I was going to like this arrangement. I was accustomed to socializing with the opposite sex. I got the impression that there was not much interaction between the boys and girls at the third-grade level. I never realized just how segregated it would get, even in the older grades. Especially in the older grades. But school attendance was always a good thing for me, no matter what was going on in my young life. I really liked school, and I didn't have to struggle to retain anything. It seemed to come easy for me. I do recall, though, studying very hard in order to get the highest grades in the class. I was able to accomplish that during my tenure at St. Hedwig. With rare exception, I was the ideal student.

It was Tuesday evening, after a supper of delicious liver, onions, and mashed potatoes. We were allowed to play outside for about an

hour when Sister Felicia summoned our class to line up in front of
the main entrance. From there we marched, column of twos, upstairs
to the dormitory. We were instructed to don our swimming trunks
and put our jeans on over them. It was bath night, and I was in for
a real experience.

Every Tuesday night was bath night for the third- and fourth-
grade boys. Exceptions were unheard of. There were four large
tubs located on the first (ground) floor of the building. These tubs
measured approximately twenty-feet by three feet and were filled
with steaming water. As we came marching in two by two, each of
us were handed a bar of soap and a washrag. We were directed into
the tub by twos until the tub was filled with about twenty boys. The
water was not hot as it looked. When the water would cool off, one
of the boys in the front would be directed to turn on the hot water
spigot, and everyone would push the hot water toward the rear of
the tub. This was when it was not such a good thing to be closest
to the spigot. That water was hot.

So far so good, I thought. But then came the "attention getter."
Sister Felicia clapped her hands in that obnoxiously loud manner,
which only she could do; and without a word being spoken,
everyone dunked their head under water. I did not feel comfortable
about making waves at this point, so I also dunked my head. Even
with my head underwater, I heard the unmistakable voice of Sister
Felicia shouting a command. I did not understand what she said,
but it meant to bring your head out of the water and start soaping
your hair. I followed suit as twenty boys in our tub were vigorously
washing their heads. Sister started with her running commentary,
telling twenty boys how to take a bath. "Soap up your washcloth and
wash the inside of your right ear. Frankie, I said, your right ear. Now
your left. Get the potatoes out. Keep washing your left ear until I tell
you to stop." Then Sister Felicia stated, "Down!" and immediately
twenty boys dunked their heads under water. After a "safe" amount
of time, I brought up my head to catch some air. *Bam!* I was caught
red-handed. Sister told me to get my head underwater with the rest
and wait for the command to come up for air. I did not argue with
her. I immediately dunked my head to await her instructions. "Up!"
Sister yelled, and twenty heads popped up from the water. Sister
continued, "Soap up those rags! Wash your neck! Mikey, wash harder.
Georgie, quit talking. Richard, stop scowling. Keep washing those

dirty necks. Now move down to your chest and stomach. Wash! Wash! Eddie, shut your mouth and keep washing. Now, wash your neighbor's back. Go on! Go on! Now switch. Quickly! Quickly!"

This went on and on until we were finished with our bath. What an experience. I never felt so clean though. "Out! Out! Out! NOW! No lingering," Sister Felicia shouted. This woman was in total control of her group. She also directed the drying procedure, including the drying of your neighbor's back. For the next two years, I was to take a bath every Tuesday without fail under the direction of Sister Felicia. When I would become a fifth-grader, all this would change. There was another "bathroom" on the same floor, several doors down, which housed approximately eight private tubs with real shower curtains. Yes sir, when you hit fifth grade, you were afforded some privacy when you took a bath.

THE GREAT ALTAR CAPER

I was still getting my feet wet in this strange place. This was my second week in the mainstream of the orphanage, and I was still learning how to find my way around the huge complex. I used the chapel as my point of reference. From the chapel, I could find most places that I needed to find. After all, we were attending church twice a day, morning and night. The morning Mass was mandatory for all students, no matter how old. The evening service was mandatory for most of us. It was October, a special month for Mary, Jesus's mother. The service didn't last more than twenty-five minutes.

It was difficult for me to make friends in this institution, at least at first, so I did a lot of roaming around. The nuns cut me some slack because they knew I was just trying to find out where different places were—that is, until the great altar caper.

I found myself in the rear of the chapel and focused on the tabernacle, that little box structure built right into the altar table. It had a single door, which was unlocked with a pretty good-sized key. The tabernacle itself measured about two by two feet. I had always wondered what they kept in it. During the actual Mass, I had observed that the priest would put the wafers and gold chalice inside and then carefully lock the door. The key would be removed and left lying on the table. In fact, I saw the key in all its glory, just waiting for me on the altar table. Curiosity got the better of me as I slowly walked up to the altar to get a better look. It was 12:45 p.m., the tail end of lunchtime, and I was due back in class at 1:00 p.m. I had time to take a look. What else was in there?

Of all the luck, there sat a small ladder at the corner of the sanctuary. Someone was in the process of cleaning the statues on either side of the altar. I moved the ladder to the center of the altar and ascended my eight-year-old body to the top step. I leaned across the table, picked up the key, and carefully examined it. The key appeared to be made of gold or gold plated. The key itself was unusually light in weight. I guess if it was real gold, they wouldn't let it lie around like that. I inserted the key into the lock, and the door popped open with a little assistance from me. I was just getting ready to take a good look inside when a woman's shrill voice startled me, causing me to lose my balance and come close to falling off the ladder.

"Just what do you think you are doing?" demanded the nun. She quickly closed the tabernacle door and locked it.

"What are you doing? Who are you? Who said you could come in here?"

"I'm sorry, Sister. I was just looking to see what was inside" was my feeble reply. I somehow found myself off the ladder and backing away from the sister. But she wasn't going to let me get away. She suddenly charged at me like a possessed person and grabbed my upper arm. She sure had a grip for an older woman. Hell, she was probably forty years old. I thought she was going to break my arm with that grip of hers. I was not about to try to escape. I was caught and had to face the music.

"We're going to the monsignor," she uttered. I am trying to figure out what a monsignor was when this very physical presence walked into the sacristy area and asked what was going on. He seemed to be larger-than-life and mean looking. He was a tall man in his fifties, wearing a black cassock. I vividly recall the cloth-covered black buttons running up and down the full length of the cassock. This man was wearing a black hat of some kind with a red furry ball on the top. I had seen that type of hat worn by the priests before and after Mass, but never during Mass. And I had never seen one with the red ball. The man also reeked from the surprisingly pleasant smell of cigar smoke. This was my introduction to Fr. Francis Rusch. Actually, he was a monsignor, but all called him "Father."

The sister explained to Father Rusch what I had done and how she had surprised me. When I saw the stern look on his face, I really got scared. I thought I was going to pee in my pants. He beckoned to me with his hand to follow him. I considered making a break for it. Neither of these people really knew who I was. I knew I could outrun this guy, but something told me to follow him and suffer the consequences. Take your punishment like a man. I did not feel good. My stomach was churning the recently ingested food I had eaten for lunch. I had hoped that I would be able to keep the food down. I did not want to piss this guy off any more than he was.

Father Rusch pointed to the chair in the sacristy and stated, "Sit down." This man was making me tremble. I had never been so scared in my short life. When he spoke, it came out as a loud, officious command. Believe me, I sat down. I even surprised myself when I sat down so hard. I definitely wanted to please this person. Then I started to shake uncontrollably. For the longest time, the monsignor said nothing. Then he spoke.

"How long have you been here at St. Hedwig?"

"Two weeks, sir."

"What grade are you in?"

"Third grade, sir. Sister Hilarion's class."

"Aren't you supposed to be in class right now?"

"Yes, sir," I stammered.

"Why were you trying to open the tabernacle? What were you going to do?"

I replied, "I just wanted to see what was kept in it. I haven't been in too many Catholic churches, and I was wondering what they kept in there. I see the priest put the Holy Communion and the wine chalice inside the tabernacle during Mass. I'm sorry, Father. I was just looking."

He beckoned me over to where he was seated on a bench, looked me in the eye, and stated, "Don't you ever do that again. The tabernacle is holy, and only a priest is allowed to touch it. Do you understand me?"

"Yes, sir. I understand."

"Let's get you back to class. You need your education. If you study hard, you can make something of your life. We reward our good students. I want you to be a good student."

"Yes, sir, I will be a good student. I promise," I replied with relief. I kept waiting to get clobbered, but it never happened. Just his voice was enough to make me cringe. I didn't ever want to make this man angry.

"Let's go," he commanded. I followed Father Rusch out of the sacristy and through the corridors of Saint Hedwig Orphanage, right to my classroom. Sister Hilarion was in the process of writing on the blackboard when we made our entrance. You could see the entire class cringe when we entered.

"Your student and I were talking, and I lost track of the time," Father Rusch stated. "Blame me for his being late. He's a good student." I suddenly realized that this rough and tough-talking man had a heart of gold. I was amazed and humbled. He let me off the hook and made it easy for me to stay in the good graces of my teacher. He probably saw the look of shock on my face as he was about to leave. We made eye contact, and he actually winked. The half smile on his face was probably only seen by me, but what a welcome sight it was. I smiled back and stated, "Thank you, Father. Thank you for everything."

Father Rusch abruptly left the classroom. Sister Hilarion never questioned me about my first meeting with Father Rusch. My classmates, however, looked upon me in awe. They seemed to think I was something special, to actually be escorted to class by the monsignor.

I'll never forget that first encounter with Monsignor Rusch. He was always a formidable presence, no matter where or when I would run into him for the next eight years. Always gruff and seemingly unsmiling, I knew he was a good guy underneath that armament of his. Yet I feared him for the duration. It was a healthy fear. It probably greatly influenced me for my entire stay at Saint Hedwig. My classmates, on the other hand, accepted the new kid quicker than most new arrivals. Many times in the next few weeks, my newly found friends and adopted family would ask me about Father Rusch and what we talked about. I never did let on what led to our meeting.

VISITING SUNDAY

The best that I can remember, "Visiting Sunday" was the second and the fourth Sunday of each month. Why they did not have each and every Sunday a Visiting Sunday was beyond me. Even in the case of the true orphans, those without mothers and fathers, there were usually some relatives who would visit them on a Visiting Sunday. When there were five Sundays in a month, it became especially hard to handle. Why couldn't the extra Sunday be a bonus Visiting Sunday? All of us looked forward to a Visiting Sunday. Visiting hours were from 1:00 p.m. until 5:00 p.m. Why not have visiting hours all day from about 10:00 a.m. to at least 6:00 p.m.? But no, the administration would only allow four precious hours.

Right after lunch and after our chores were done, everyone was directed to their respective dayroom. There was usually a small television set in each dayroom. The smaller kids, up to and including fourth grade, had virtually no place to sit except on the floor. There may have been a couch at the back of the room for those grades, but no one used it. The television screens were rather small, and if one sat on the couch, it would be difficult to make out what was occurring on the television program. I recall that fifth and sixth grades had the same setup as the others, but there were more couches available. Some of the fifth- and sixth-graders actually used the couches. The guys who had the best dayroom were the seventh- and eighth-graders. Their dayroom was the largest (at least on the boy's side) and had the most furniture. It was a very comfortable room, airy and bright. Their dayroom had a console radio. If one wanted to watch television, however, there was one available in the room next door. Unless there was a Chicago Cubs game on television, there wasn't much television watching when one got to seventh and eighth grades. Those guys were content to listen to popular music. The younger grades watched Mary Hartline of the *Super Circus* and the *Morris B. Sachs Amateur Hour*. There wasn't much choice. I seem to remember that whoever appeared on the *Amateur Hour* and played "Lady of Spain" on the accordion won the top prize.

Each Visiting Sunday, all of us spent the afternoon in our respective dayroom. No one was allowed on the playground. No one was allowed to play baseball. In fact, we were required to wear our Sunday best the entire day, whether or not we were expecting visitors. It was a long day for those kids who didn't get visitors. I remember there were a lot of those kids. Some would sit in a corner and cry. Others would just sit and go through the motions of watching a program on TV. Others were just openly hostile toward whoever got in their way. I remember one kid, about twelve or thirteen years old, sitting on a couch, going through a comic book, flipping pages. You could just feel the tension emitting from his body. He obviously was hoping someone, anyone, would come to visit him this day. One o'clock came and several of his classmates were called down to the office, the indication that someone had come to visit them. Two o'clock came and other classmates were called down. You could just see the anxiety building in this kid. About 2:15 p.m., the boy who had office duty, going to the respective dayrooms and escorting kids to the office, entered our dayroom and called this kid's name. The tension left his face in a second as he broke into a huge grin. "Hot dog. I got visitors," he said to no one in particular. He almost broke into a run as he left the dayroom for the quick trip down the stairs to the office where his visitors were waiting for him.

SORRY, SISTER

Growing up in the late forties left some indelible memories. It was shortly after World War II. President Harry S. Truman was getting his feet wet as an elected president of our great country. I was in the third grade, living in a brand-new home (again) called St. Hedwig Industrial School for Boys. At least that was the name listed on some of the old postcards, which were available in the administrative offices. In reality, the more popular name was St. Hedwig Orphanage. The institution did have its own shoe shop, which was located on the bottom floor of a four-story building. However, the shop had not been in use for several years.

My dormitory was located on the third floor. It was a large room, probably fifty by thirty feet. There were twenty-four cots arranged in three rows. Between the beds was a nondescript bedside cabinet. It had a drawer, which held one's personal effects such as a comb, toothbrush, soap, baseball mitt (if you were lucky enough to have one), checkers set, or pencils. The lower part was used for your underwear. Most of the clothing, including one's pants, was stored neatly in the adjoining walk-in closet located adjacent to the nun's private room. The nun's room, referred to as a cell, was an eight-by-ten-foot room housing a cot-type bed (better than ours) and her own sink with hot and cold running water.

Sister Felicia, who was my dormitory nun in the third and fourth grades, towered over us kids. She seemed to be at least six feet tall, skinny, and walked with a limp. She was a formidable supervisor who had no difficulty getting your attention. Most of the time, she was a dear old soul. Every once in a while, someone would suffer from the wrath of this woman. In some ways, she was like a saint. In other ways, she proved that she was a human being capable of making mistakes. I had always tried to be on her good side. We all did.

One of her chores was dealing with one of my classmates, Joe Koski. Joe was an eight-year-old who happened to wet the bed on occasion. Over the years, doctors and medical science have discovered the root of this malady and have developed medications to cope with it. Unfortunately, that was not the belief during those days.

Each morning, Sister Felicia would awaken us with the loud, thunderous clapping of her hands. I never did get used to it. I would fly out of bed and almost run to the bathroom with toothbrush in hand. That was my cue. The slower kids had to wait for a sink or share one. I almost never had to share one. There were approximately twenty sinks available for two classes, third and fourth grades. With approximately twenty-five boys per class, things got a bit crowded.

On one occasion, shortly after my arrival at St. Hedwig, when I got back to my bed, I immediately dressed and made up the bed. That's when I noticed Sister Felicia chewing out Joe. Apparently, Joe had wet the bed on this occasion and was in the process of removing his soiled sheets for transportation to the skunk room. The skunk room was where all the bed wetters took their soiled sheets. I continued with the making of my bed when I heard a resounding slap. I looked up and saw that Joe had been knocked off balance by this apparent blow. He must have given the wrong answer to Sister Felicia's question. All I heard Joe say was "Sorry, Sister."

On many occasions, I noted that seven or eight bed wetters from other classes were forced to march to the dining room where the rest of us were eating breakfast. They were joined by the girl bed wetters on those occasions. The bed wetters had to don their soiled, wet sheets hanging around their necks. They were made to stand at the front of the dining room for all to see. At that time, I did not think that was right. I was just extremely glad that I was not a bed wetter. On occasion, I would experience nightmares about wetting the bed. Thank God I never did. Exposing these children to the general population in this manner was not a good thing in my humble opinion. These poor guys were not allowed breakfast until the dining room emptied of the other students. Sadly, boys and girls who wet the bed were treated the same. Public ridicule and punishment were the norm.

On one occasion, I had observed Joe being violently smacked with a belt on his behind by one of the nuns. At other times, he was treated with much kindness and understanding. I never could figure it out. I was just a kid anyway and not expected to understand these things. But I knew that it was not right to punish these poor unfortunates.

I vividly recall Joe and the others being the subject of some kind of experiment. Some visiting doctor had devised a contraption to supposedly prevent bed-wetting. It consisted of two empty spools of thread and some heavy-duty twine connecting them. This device was wrapped around one's waist just prior to bedtime. How was one to get any sleep with this contraption in place? I guess that was the idea, not to get a good night's sleep so you can visit the toilet when needed. After all, some of the nuns seemed to think that bed wetters were lazy.

It was tough growing up in those times, especially if you were a bed wetter. I have found out though that so-called normal parents in the world outside the confines of the orphanage treated their bed-wetting children just as the nuns did and punished them. Some of the punishments were humane, yet some seemed to be on the sadistic side.

In recent years, I have had occasion to communicate with several of those bed wetters who had been in my class. For the most part, the deep, emotional scars have been healed, thanks to counseling. Yet not one of them will ever forget the shoddy treatment they received during those years. Joe won't forget. When I first spoke to Joe as an adult, he seemed to be a very negative, uptight individual. He distinctly remembered the shame and embarrassment of being a bed wetter. He once asked me if he was the only one who remembered the treatment of bed wetters at St. Hedwig Orphanage. I assured him that I did remember how they were treated. His recollection was a lot more vivid than mine. Our discussion was what helped jog my memory to write about the treatment of bed wetters at St. Hedwig Orphanage.

MERRY, MERRY CHRISTMAS

It was December 1950. Christmas was just around the corner. All of us kids were assembled in the gymnasium to practice the singing of Christmas carols. There were probably five hundred of us, ranging anywhere between ages five and sixteen. We were required to sit on the metal folding chairs in that cold, cold gym and belt out the songs of the season with feelings. That was tough to do. The music director insisted we practice until we got it right. One of the new songs that year, if I've got it right, was "Rudolph the Red-Nosed Reindeer" by Gene Autry. Another newcomer was "Frosty the Snowman." Sister Charisima was the nun in charge of the assembly. Being the resident music teacher, she played the piano and tried to lead the gathering in voice. Let's face it, some of us just did not have our heart in it. This was the third assembly this week, and it was getting old.

In several days, the American Legion was going to make their annual appearance at St. Hedwig Orphanage, and the orphans traditionally entertained the legion with Christmas carols. The legion, after listening to the carols for about an hour, would put on their own show. I had no idea what a delight it would be. We had to practice for the legion, and we had to get the songs right. Sister Charisima decided that it was not going to get any better and so informed us. Reluctantly, she dismissed the horde for lunch and, with a sigh, informed the mother superior that the children were as ready as their ability permitted.

The big day arrived, and assembly in the gymnasium was set for 7:00 p.m. There was a certain amount of excitement in the air and much talk among the older children, those with a couple of Christmases under their belt at St. Hedwig. The main topic of discussion was that the Christmas presents would be passed around by the American Legion personnel. The chief complaint I picked up on was that the American Legion had been giving brand-new checkers sets to the seventh and eighth grades three years running. They all seemed to think that checkers sets would once again be distributed to the seventh and eighth grades. I was in the fourth grade, so I was not too concerned about what I would get from the American Legion.

The gymnasium was filled with children, much more than for the Christmas carol practice. Upon closer inspection, I noted that there were a lot of "outsider" guests, adults. They seemed to be more excited than the children. I don't think they were scheduled to receive any gifts from the legion, but they still seemed to be on edge, waiting for something special to happen.

The gathering of the St. Hedwig Orphanage children broke out with "O Little Town of Bethlehem," accompanied by Mr. Joe Skubish on the organ. Joe was our music director. I never heard that song sound so good. Maybe it was the accompaniment of the organ, but these kids really sounded good. They put a lot of feeling into their singing. Then came "Jolly Ole St. Nick" and "The First Noel." We really belted out the tunes and sounded good. Sister Charisima looked so proud. There she stood, at the front of the auditorium, regally conducting the five hundred or so voices. She seemed so pleased. It was a sight to behold. I even felt a little twitter in my heart. The music sounded so harmonious. I supposed that this is what is meant by "with feeling." This joyful singing went on for about an hour.

Finally, after the last notes of "Silent Night" floated away, someone, as if on cue, turned on all the lights of the gymnasium. Suddenly, from the double doors at the rear of the assembly, came the sound of a drumbeat. It was merely a drumbeat, but it sent shivers up and down my spine. The doors flew open, and the Niles contingent of the American Legion began to proudly march into the auditorium. They were about thirty strong in all. There were five snare drummers, one base drummer, and the rest carried a bugle. All marched in perfect time. Most of the bugles were highly polished brass. I noted that there were also a few trumpets in the group. They marched up the center aisle of the auditorium, column of twos, smartly marching to the beat of the drums. As they reached the front of the auditorium, they peeled off to the right and left and finally ascended the steps at the right and left of the gigantic stage. They did this with precise military steps, marching to their position on the stage. They continued marching in place until the last member arrived in place. They may have been wearing ragtag uniforms, but I thought they were the sharpest military group I had ever seen.

The marching stopped abruptly, and the appreciative audience showed their enthusiasm by clapping their hands. The leader of the band turned and faced the assembly, bowed, did an about-face, held up his bandleader's wand, and the drum and bugle corps began their litany of songs. Memory fails me, but I seem to recall that they played numerous marches like only a drum and bugle corps could do. A few Christmas songs were interspersed to add spice to the throng of music lovers. Then suddenly the music was over. The band marched off the stage and exited the gym through the center aisle, just like their entry. Here again, the instep marching was done so professionally as a single unit; this nine-year-old was never more impressed by anything he had ever seen. That drumbeat really did it. I had never been to a parade in my life, and I imagined that this was the closest thing to it. I had heard about parades and even read about them in books, but I had never experienced music like this. My love for music was riled up on this occasion and has stayed with me throughout my life. To this day, I especially love marching music.

Several of the uniformed members of the drum and bugle corps reentered the gymnasium and walked to the front of the building. They strategically placed themselves at the front of the stage and began to remove white sheets, which had been covering about five ten-foot-long tables. Atop the tables were numerous Christmas presents: dolls, toy cars, toy trucks, checkers, Chinese checkers, paddleballs (a small paddle attached to a little rubber ball with a rubber band) and candy. There were bags and bags of hard candy. To this day, I refer to hard candy as "Christmas" candy.

Next came the dispensing of the presents. The nuns had done this before. It was run like a military operation. Every nun knew her job. Class by class was brought up to the front of the gym. Each student was to be given their individual gift. When it came time for the third- and fourth-graders to walk up to the front of the gym, we were all wondering out loud what the verdict would be. Who was going to get what? With mixed emotions, the first member of our class accepted his checkers set. Then the second and the third and so forth. I walked up to the dispenser of the checkers and asked for a paddleball. Two of the nuns swooped down on me and were getting ready to remove me from the premises when the bandleader interceded and said, "Let him have the paddleball. We have enough." The two nuns reluctantly let me go. I grasped the paddleball and returned to my seat with my class. The rest of my class was already seated with their checker sets in their lap. I got the strangest looks from my peers when I sat down. I am sure they were all thinking, "How does he rate? Why should he be different?"

After all the presents were given out, the organ began playing the "Thank You" song. The entire student body joined in and sang it loud and raucous. Then starting with the "young kids,"—preschoolers—the auditorium was systematically evacuated. Each class would walk by a table laden with Christmas candy, and a bag of the precious stuff would be handed to each person as they left the building. As our class walked out of the gymnasium, two of the nuns literally "mugged me" for my paddleball. One of them sneered, "Now you got nothing. Just what you deserve, you selfish brat."

I was not that upset that the paddleball was taken from me. I was still high from the music I had heard that evening. Besides, my classmates all had checkers sets. It takes two to play checkers, doesn't it? I smiled as I marched with my class for the return to the dormitory. I could almost hear the drummer as my feet were keeping in step-one, two, one, two.

CAMP VILLA MARIE

Those first few years at St. Hedwig were so precious. There were so many new and exciting experiences. So much was going on in my life that it made the transition from "normal life" to "orphan life" so much easier. There were a lot of distractions. This kept me from dwelling on my precarious predicament. Why was I here? What did I do? Why me?

One of these distractions was the privilege of going to camp. In these modern times that we now live in, summer camp is made available not only to the wealthier families, but also to the not-so-fortunate families. In Los Angeles, California, there is an annual fund-raising drive sponsored by the *Los Angeles Times* newspaper that collects thousands of dollars to put a less fortunate child in camp for one week. Back in the late forties and fifties, Catholic Charities operated a summer camp called Camp Villa Marie. The camp, which was exclusively intended for children incarcerated in orphanages, was located off Pistakee Bay in McHenry County, Illinois, in the southeast part of Johnsburg. It is part of the Fox Lake waterways.

It was about a two-hour bus ride from St. Hedwig to Camp Villa Marie, especially on those rickety old school buses. Everyone on the bus knew they were going to camp, and the excitement continued unabated. Everyone on the bus participated in singing every song they knew. One of the mandatory songs was "One Hundred Bottles of Beer on the Wall." It was sung with gusto. When the bus finally reached Camp Villa Marie and began the descent down the narrow driveway, the jubilation was rampant. Everyone was excited. Yes, even the nuns. Maybe they were just so glad the noisy bus trip was over.

The older kids stayed in cinder block buildings toward the top of the hill of the complex. All the rest of the kids and nuns stayed in the barracks-style buildings in the main section of the camp, seemingly surrounding the dining room. After all, the dining room was the center of activity. Thinking back, the entire camp reminded me of Camp Leonard Wood, Missouri, where basic training for new soldiers is conducted by the U.S. Army. Camp Villa Marie was a lot more pleasant.

As structured as our life was at St. Hedwig (church seven days a week was the norm), life at camp was totally unstructured. At camp, you did not have to attend church services every day except on Sunday. One of my classmates, Ron Weiss, never missed a day at church. We considered him "the Saint." I suppose each class had a student who fit that description during those days. I attended Mass one day just to get the attention of the nuns who knew me. I don't know who most of the nuns were that day, but no one noticed me attending church in the middle of the week at camp. I was so disappointed. The much-needed brownie points just were not available that day.

There was no set time for breakfast. You could sleep for as long as you desired. The meal was served between 6:30 and 8:30 a.m., or something close to it. We kids were allowed to wander into breakfast when we felt like it. Talk about living in heaven, it was wonderful. The other meals were more structured, but after hours of physical activity, we were ready to eat. There didn't seem to be any objection from any of the kitchen staff if someone happened to wander into the kitchen during the day for a snack. One of the cooks actually fried up one of my buddy's freshly caught fish. That must have been a treat. I never seemed to have any luck at catching fish, something that has followed me into my adult life.

While at camp, the nuns seemed to take a backseat and let the counselors run everything. The camp counselors were young adults, both male and female, who were involved with Catholic Charities. The males were usually brothers or brothers in training. A brother was the same as a sister or nun, one step short of the priesthood. These guys were great. The boys all fell in love with the female counselors, which were few and far between. The counselors spent some structured time with appointed grades throughout the day. The day's activities of the camp were posted by the dining room. It was a must to know what was scheduled for that particular day. I used to check the list before breakfast and report back to my friends. Participation was usually not mandatory, except on rare occasions.

Ping-Pong and volleyball were two of the main activities. There was an old upright piano in the dayroom that was very popular with the kids. My good friend, Russ Lukes, got pretty good with some of the old favorites like "Heart and Soul," "Peg O' My Heart," and "On Top of Old Smokey." There were also day hikes to Chapel Hill and into the city of Johnsburg, an old-time German community. The camp had a large coast guard-type boat, which was named "the Ark." It held about thirty kids and several adults. The hour-long boat ride to some distant shore was usually the highlight of the week. I tasted my first grilled hamburger on one of these outings. The counselors would fire up a barbecue grill and start cooking. That first grilled hamburger was one of the most delicious meals I have ever had. I will never forget it.

Fishing could be done at any time. In fact, some of us more daring types would get up at four in the morning and go fishing. We had to check our "night lines" for catfish. I never caught anything, but one of my classmates, Joe Plachy, sure did. That kid knew how to fish. Later in the day, we could then take a nap if we were tired. Such a life!

The evening was usually filled with group activities. The campfire was the gathering place for most of the events. Sometimes we even had a weenie roast and a marshmallow roast immediately following. One of my favorites was gathering around the campfire and listening to scary stories from the counselors. One of the classics that I remember was the story of Max the Sacks. This degenerate allegedly lived on a nearby island and protected his realm with a bloodied ax in one hand and a burlap sack in the other. We used to wonder what was kept in the sack. Heaven help the wayward boater who happened to land on his island, or so the legend said. This story would be repeated each year. The counselors would improvise and improve on it each time it was told. It made for great entertainment.

At some point during the evening, we would all sing songs. Occasionally, there would be a movie shown outdoors. On one occasion, the counselors had filled a large washtub with water and one gallon of gasoline. The gasoline stayed on top of the water. Another counselor went to the roof of the adjacent building with a six-inch doll in his hand. He affixed a parachute to the doll, told the other counselor to ignite the gasoline, and then tossed the doll toward the inferno. What an impression that must have made on the younger kids in attendance. He missed and missed. When the parachute finally did land in the tub, the fire had gone out.

One night, the featured entertainment was boxing. The counselors put up a legitimate boxing ring, and the whole camp population attended. I guess every one likes a fight. Many of the kids had signed up earlier to fight one another. Most of the fights were over within a minute. Whoever got the first punch was the winner when the recipient of the punch broke out crying. Then the bigger kids got into the act. The three-round bouts were interesting. Some of the guys merely danced around the ring and tried to make it look like they knew something about boxing. Others went after each other with a vengeance, pounding away. It was not pretty. Then they ran out of opponents and were looking toward the audience for more participants. A friend of mine, whom I will call Lenny, asked me to box with him. Lenny was almost half my size despite the fact he was a classmate of mine. I reluctantly agreed after listening to his plea. He promised to box and block. I did likewise. After we started sparring, most of the kids in attendance started yelling and booing. They wanted blood. Lenny started picking up his punches. God, he could really hit for such a little guy. After about the third solid hit in my face, I got a little upset with him. He reneged on his promise, so I charged him like a rhino. After about fifteen consecutive hits on his face, Father Bill wisely stepped in and stopped the fight. This was a perfect example of a mob dictating how a fight was to be done. I was declared the winner by TKO. This was obviously not one of my prouder moments. Lenny never held it against me though.

Each year, the camp was populated by different grades at different times. It was rare that the female members of my class or anyone close to their age were at camp the same time that I was. There was some sort of a definitive segregation of the sexes that really affected me. I always had an eye for the older girls but can remember only one time that the older girls attended camp the same week that I did. I must have been very young that year because as we got older, the boys and girls were always segregated and not allowed to attend camp at the same time. Maybe that's why camp lost its appeal for me when I got into high school. After our week at camp was up, we reluctantly boarded the convoy of school buses for the long ride back to Chicago. Those return trips were unusually quiet. Everybody was sad. The length of time spent at camp went by so quickly. Every Hedwigian I have ever talked to in recent years has very fond memories of Camp Villa Marie. We were so fortunate.

Ms. Gen Nolan, who used to be the director of the camp, made it all happen. She is in her eighties now. She retired to the Downers Grove area of Illinois. Thanks, Gen. You did a great job. You helped make a lot of kids happy way back then. God bless you for all your efforts.

BEST FRIENDS

It was the start of a new school year. We were well within the month of September 1949, fourth grade, and the teacher was Sister Mary Christiana. I have fond memories of Sister Christiana. I was a good student, and she liked good students. It was such a positive experience for me. She was one of the first nuns to note that I was an exceptional student who needed just a bit of prodding. In fact, she was the nun who helped me win my first writing contest. The topic was "What Good Citizenship Means to Me." The contest was sponsored by one of the local Chicago radio stations. I actually won two radios: one for my class and one for myself. This was a big deal in 1949. Not every classroom had its own radio, let alone your own personal radio.

There was a new student assigned to our class. His name was Russ Lukes. Many years later, I found that his original Polish name was Lukaszewski. Could you imagine going through life with a name like that? Ouch! Russ seemed to be a nice guy, and I took an immediate liking to him. As was customary, all the other kids in my class ignored Russ that first week. Being the ornery person that I had chosen to be during that period, I took Russ under my wing. The hell with tradition. The way he remembers it though is that I resented him for whatever reason and beat the living daylights out of him. That's not really what occurred, at least not the way I remember it.

Sister Christiana was giving us our math lesson for the day. It was about 10:30 a.m. All eyes were on the teacher when all of a sudden, Russ threw up his breakfast. This offensive barrage landed right smack in the middle of his desk. Unfortunately, his math book was the target of attack. The sister motioned for Russ to leave the room and directed me to assist him in any way I could after I cleaned up the vomit. The smell was odorous. I objected to Sister Christiana. "Why me?" Sister took great relish in telling me that Russ was my friend. I muttered something about life not being fair and dutifully cleaned up the mess. It was the grossest thing I had ever done. It wasn't even my own puke. I then went to the restroom down the hall and caught up with my friend.

"What do you want?" was the first thing out of his mouth. I could not believe his attitude. Here I was trying to help him and he gives me a hard time. I told him that the nun insisted I accompany him to make sure he is all right. If there was a fight, it probably happened at this point. We were both a little testy. I made a point of letting him know who cleaned up his mess. I never did let him forget that incident. How was I to know that our lives would undergo some unbelievable parallels in the decades that followed? What a way to bond a friendship. For the next seven years, Russ and I did just about everything together.

In 1956, I left St. Hedwig Orphanage for reasons that I will discuss later in this book. Russ left about a month after I did. We lost contact after those first few months of freedom. We did not talk to each other or associate with each other for the next twenty-eight years or so. Fortunately, Russ attended a reunion of St. Hedwig Alumni in 1984. He spotted a woman wearing a name tag that caused his heart to jump. After some discussion with this woman, he discovered that it was my sister, Sandra. He obtained my address and telephone number from her, wrote me a letter, and we continued the relationship to this present day. We filled in the gaps pretty quickly.

In our correspondence with each other, I found out that Russ joined the U.S. Army and took his basic training at Fort Leonard Wood, Missouri, in July 1958. Unbeknownst to him, I joined the U.S. Army in July of 1958 and was also sent to Fort Leonard Wood for my basic training. He was two weeks ahead of me, stationed in a barracks not more than one hundred yards from my barracks. Yet neither of us knew the other was so close. He was a reservist. I was part of the regular army. He put in six months. I put in three years. Who was the smarter of the two?

Russ finished his six-month tour of duty with the U.S. Army and launched himself into civilian life. I had a three-year commitment to the army, so I had to make the best of a bad decision. I never knew you could become a reservist. Why hadn't someone told me? I didn't have a clue.

On April 8, 1961, Russ married his high school sweetheart in Chicago. On April 13, that same year, I married my first real girlfriend in Zurich, Switzerland. Interesting, huh? Not even a week apart.

On March 5, 1962, Russ entered the academy of the Chicago Police Department. I decided to join the Los Angeles Police Department after working for a year in a flour mill. I joined on April 29, 1962. When Russ and I discussed these parallels, both of us were visibly shaken. But there's more.

The last police district that Russ worked for the past ten years was Albany Park, also known as District 17. The last police division that I had worked for almost twenty years was Devonshire Division. You guessed it, Devonshire was also known as Division 17. The parallels in our lives have been incredible. It unnerves us each time we get together to talk about the good old days. Scary stuff.

Russ retired from the Chicago Police Department January 16, 1996. I retired from the LAPD on June 16, 1990. I guess the parallels have finally run their course. However, Russ had two boys, one of which was born on February 27, 1962. My son was born on February 26, 1963. Russ's other boy was born August 30, 1963. My daughter was born October 6, 1961. There sure are a lot of sixes involved.

To this day, Russ and I are the best of friends. We continue to get together to relive our time in St. Hedwig Orphanage. Between us, we did not come up with a whole lot of negative experiences. We firmly believe that our time spent at St. Hedwig helped us to cope with a not-always-predictable existence in the real world. It made us what we are today. Sister Marcy, are you listening?

WRIGLEY FIELD, CIRCA 1950

I had been at St. Hedwig a couple of years and was busy making my mark. I had excelled in my studies to the point that the teachers did notice me. There were fringe benefits to be had, and I wanted to experience them. Last year's boat trip was a very enjoyable experience. An acquaintance of Monsignor Rusch owned a thirty-six-foot cabin cruiser. This benefactor made it possible for the two highest-scoring students in each class, grades 3 through 8, to enjoy a day away from the orphanage on a boat large enough to accommodate a large group. There were twelve students and two chaperoning nuns on that trip. We put away countless bags of potato chips and soda pop. I am sure there was a meal thrown in, but I don't recall the details. The boat took us on a trip across Lake Michigan, which lasted several hours. It was an unforgettable experience. Scholastic standing meant something in this place, and I wanted to cash in on it. Unbeknownst to me, the reward for my fourth-grade achievements was to outdo the boat trip.

Ron Weiss, the tallest kid in our class, accompanied me on the boat trip. He finished just behind me in scholastic standing that year. We were summoned from our classroom by Sister Christiana. She was our fourth-grade teacher, and I really liked her. She informed us that once again, Ron and I had earned a special reward for our good grades during the school year. Even though it was the last week of school for the semester, Ron and I looked forward to an outing, anything away from the orphanage. But we both were stunned when informed that Father Bill was going to take us to the Chicago Cubs baseball game that afternoon. Ron and I were the only kids in the school who were lucky enough to be selected. Father Bill was the youngest of the three priests assigned to St. Hedwig, and the nicest. Also going to the game with us was a good friend of Father Bill's, Jules Pandera. The kids who did not know better called Jules "Father Juice." Ron and I were thrilled to be included in such select company. Jules was probably my first conscious male role model. Even though he was a "product" of St. Hedwig, he never forgot where his "home" was. While a member of the student body of St. Hedwig, probably ten years earlier, he was a basketball and a baseball star. The man was a natural athlete. Many a time he would play with us kids, teaching us the finer points of basketball and baseball. He preferred associating with the older high school kids, but it was not beneath him to play with us younger kids. He was a great coach.

Ron Weiss and I were instructed to wait for Father Bill and Jules in the parking area below the chapel. Game time was 1:00 p.m., and it was now 11:30 a.m. Suddenly, we saw the two men approaching. Ron poked me in the ribs and stated, "Isn't this great? We're gonna see the Cubs play." I slapped him on the back and reminded him, "Yeah, but they're playing the Brooklyn Dodgers, my favorite." Both of us were in the early stages of heaven. What an experience!

When we arrived at Wrigley Field, the four of us walked rapidly toward the main gate off Sheffield Avenue. Jules handed each of us our ticket and admonished us, "Hang on to it. Don't lose it." We walked into the confines of the ballpark and began ascending the ramp toward the interior of the stadium. We turned a corner and there, right in front of my eyes, was the most beautiful baseball diamond I had ever seen. I felt like I was in a dream. The green grass was so vibrant and alive. The white bases were so white and clean. The outfield wall was covered with luscious green ivy. Batting practice had just concluded, and the grounds crew was smoothing the infield with their landscape rakes. One of the crew members lifted up second base and attached a water hose to the water spigot concealed underneath. He then sprayed a fine mist over the entire dirt portion of the infield. Father Bill led us to our seats right on the first base side between home and first base, just behind the

Dodger dugout. Jules handed me a program so that I could follow the lineup and keep score. I was elated. The leadoff batter for the Dodgers listed in the lineup was Pee Wee Reese. Jackie Robinson was also playing, along with Gil Hodges, Billy Cox, Carl Furillo, and Roy "Campy" Campanella. I don't remember any of the other players for the Dodgers. The Cubs featured Hank Sauer in left field, Andy Pafko in center, Phil Cavaretta at first base, Roy Smally at shortstop, and I believe Johnny Klippstein was pitching.

I don't know who won that day, and I didn't care. It was one of the most exciting days of my tender, young life. Hank Sauer hit a home run into the left-field bleachers. Andy Pafko stole second base. But who I remember the best was Campy, fouling off many pitches, running full bore toward first base, only to be called back because the ball went foul, sweat streaming down his brown face. I was so close to him I thought I could reach out and touch him. I was in total awe. About the fourth time he ran toward first base and was called back, I heard the frustration in his voice when he uttered, "Nuts." No profanity from this big leaguer. A real class act. Campy made an impression on me that day. For a long while, my favorite expression was "Nuts" when things did not go my way.

Years later, when I would coach my son's baseball team and my daughter's softball team, I tried to instill in them the same classy approach to the game as Mr. Campanella displayed on that wonderful day so many years ago. I never looked at the sport as just a game anymore. It was not important who won but how the game was played. Learn how to lose, with class.

FRIDAY-NIGHT FIGHTS

Some of my scariest times at St. Hedwig occurred during the fifth and sixth grades. Kids at that age are so vulnerable and most impressionable. Events occurred during those times that have stayed with me to this day. One of those events occurred while I was in the fifth grade. I had been watching my p's and q's and was even attempting to stay on the good side of the nuns. I recall that it was early in the school year and the leaves were starting to turn, probably mid-October.

It was shortly after "lights out" on a Friday night. Most of us were starting to doze off when I heard voices coming from down the corridor outside our dormitory. Two nuns were approaching our room, talking loudly. After all these years, I can still remember who they were. They entered our sleeping quarters and flipped on the overhead lights. This was most unusual because neither of these nuns had anything to do with the dormitory area of our floor. Sister A walked up to each cot so she could examine who was in it. When she reached Donny's bed, the nun grabbed the sleeping Donny by his arm and yanked him to a standing position.

In the meantime, all of us were starting to wake up. We were curious. What was all the commotion? Sister B ordered everyone to close their eyes and go back to sleep. She said that it was not our concern and to keep our eyes shut. That comment really got our attention.

Sister A firmly held on to Donny's arm, yelling at him in the process. "You are gonna get yours. You'll see who is the boss. We are gonna teach you a lesson you won't forget, you little brat."

These were not very loving words. What was going on? Sister B turned off the overhead lights and told everyone, "Go to sleep." Tough to do under the circumstances since both the nuns were now holding on to the struggling Donny, yelling at him. They reminded him what a rotten kid he was. They dragged his struggling body down the hall. Every once in a while, you could hear a solid slap to the face. At least I thought it was a slap. The noise of the nuns and Donny was fading as they took him up a flight of stairs to their destination, the sewing room.

Then the beating started. All of us kids could hear Donny pleading for the nuns not to hit him anymore. He was making promises to be good and that he would never sass a nun again. About this time, we boys could hear the sewing room windows being slammed shut. Apparently, they did not want the rest of the kids to hear what was going on, but they were too late. We could faintly hear Donny's screams as the nuns beat him with a wooden hand brush. We found out from Donny later that they were very indiscriminate as to where on his body they struck him. Totally exhausted, Donny ceased struggling and just laid on the floor. The nuns lost interest in beating him after a few minutes. I suppose it's not fun to beat someone who does not struggle.

About an hour later, Donny returned to his bed. I didn't think anybody was asleep. We all asked Donny if he was all right, but he just kept whimpering. The sad part was that neither of these nuns was responsible for us boys at that time of the night. Our housekeeping nun, whose private room was adjacent to the dormitory we were in, apparently slept through that racket.

HARD REALITY

We were heavily involved in our baseball game. I'm not sure what the score was, but it was close. Each side would score a run. The inning would change. Next side up would score a run. This went on and on for hours. This was not unusual at St. Hedwig. We all took our baseball seriously. And we were all pretty close in talent. Each team had their losers, but each team also had their star players. It made for good and healthy competition.

I had made the last out for our side in the prior inning, so I decided to take a quick pee. The rest rooms were about seventy-five feet away from the ball diamond, located within the first floor of the main building. It was a large rest room, probably sixty by thirty feet. On the far wall stood a line of ten or twelve toilets, each partitioned by false marble on each side and the back. The toilets faced the far wall so that the back side of the toilets faced toward the entrance of the room. There was only one kid in the toilet area, sitting in stall number five, almost directly in the middle of the line of toilets. I walked into the toilet area and proceeded toward the last stall. I heard a loud, raucous individual of about fifteen years of age come romping into the room. He turned the corner, saw the small boy seated in number five, made eye contact with me, said nothing, and proceeded to take out his penis. What he did next shocked me. He walked over to stall number five and proceeded to urinate all over the five-year-old boy. The boy could do nothing but sit. The jerk actually tried to pee in the little guy's mouth. The look of pain on that boy's face haunts me to this day. I was only nine at that time, so I could not realistically be his savior. I did recognize that something a lot more serious would have happened if I did not stick around. As uncomfortable as I was, I continued to stand there, staring straight ahead. The strangest feeling hit me. I see nothing. I hear nothing. I know nothing. This fifteen-year-old asshole should get his ass kicked by someone. What the hell is his problem? That was one time in my life I wished I was about six feet tall and strong as an ox.

After the fifteen-year-old verbally taunted the little one for a minute or two, he decided to leave the restroom. I immediately went over to the crying five-year-old. What else could I do for him other than help wipe him off with toilet paper. The poor thing was soaked in urine, and the smell was atrocious. He even had urine in his hair. I helped the five-year-old get dressed and walked him out of the restroom area where I immediately informed the nun on duty what had happened. She asked me who the older kid was, but I could not help her. I had no idea. He was in one of the higher grades, probably high school. This was my second year at St. Hedwig, and I still did not know who all the players were. So the nun climbs my frame as if it was my fault. She orders me to accompany the kid to his dormitory and help him find clean clothes. This I did without any argument. I did not make any friends with the guys I was playing baseball with. They were wondering what happened to their left fielder. The poor kid needed a bath and a shampoo. The clean clothes were only a temporary fix. Oh well. Not my problem. I should have never stuck my nose into that kid's business. But who knows what else would have happened to him. I did not know all that much about child molesters then, but I knew trouble when it happened. I'm a survivor, remember.

Three years later, after the administration had hired the fifteen-year-old as a "worker," I got even with him for what he had done to that five-year-old. So the bad boy was now eighteen years old and had his own private room in the "workers' quarters," located above the laundry toward the rear of the chapel building. He had dropped out of high school because he chose not to apply himself. Maybe it was not interesting enough for him. The orphanage administration hired him to do menial chores around the grounds. He seemed to pay particular attention to the younger boys he came across. I never saw him do anything to arouse suspicion, but I knew in my mind that he was capable of molesting youngsters. In my mind, he was the vilest creature on earth, and he was going to pay the price. This twelve-year-old was going to initiate some "payback."

One summer day, I saw him leave his private room in a hurry. I was hoping luck would be on my side. I had previously tried to get into his private room on several occasions, but his door was locked with a big padlock. I just happened to be in the right place at the right time on this occasion. It did not seem like he had time to lock his door, but I was not sure. After I followed him to his jobsite, about a half block away, I hurried back to the workers' quarters and walked straight to his room. The padlock was in the open position, inviting me into the room. I did not hesitate to enter. He forgot to lock his door. There did not appear to be anyone in the vicinity to observe me enter the room. This was my lucky day, not his. The room was not much bigger than the typical cell that the nuns lived in, probably eight by ten feet. He had a footlocker at the foot of the bed with a large padlock attached to the hasp. It would probably take dynamite to remove that lock. There wasn't enough time to try and break the padlock. It was the biggest one I had ever seen. Instead, I looked around the room. Just being in that room made me feel creepy. He must have been a creep for me to feel that way. What was I to do? This was my big chance. I checked under his mattress and found a magazine with pictures of naked men. I did not even want to touch the magazine and was about to rip it up when it hit me. Poetic justice? Yes. He'll never know what hit him. I unzipped my pants, took out my penis and urinated on his bed. I gave that blanket a good soaking, believe me. I especially concentrated on his pillow. The bed was wallowing in urine. It soaked into the mattress.

Now it was time to get out of there without being seen. I cracked the door a bit, looked down the corridor, and saw and heard nothing. It was time to move out. I slithered out of the room, down the hall, and took the stairs to the basement three at a time. Once I got to the basement, I knew I was home free. No one would be able to tie me to the newly urinated room. Gotcha, you son of a bitch. I was in an exceptional mood for the rest of the day. Even the cold hot dogs and potato salad for dinner could not ruin my day. It wasn't until years later that I ever told anyone about that incident.

As it turned out, about ten years later, this fine young man was arrested by the Chicago Police Department for molesting a young boy in the forest preserve on Milwaukee Avenue. The last I heard, he was a guest at the state penitentiary in Joliet, Illinois. Good riddance to that jerk.

DEMON ALCOHOL

I remember an incident that occurred when I was probably in the sixth grade. That would have made me about eleven or twelve years old. I had been summoned by Father Ed to accompany him to the drafting room to play my harmonica. For some reason, he thought it was really neat that I could play any song I put my mind to, as long as I knew the melody. I taught myself to play the harmonica. I even thought I was pretty good at it. He would ask me to play simple tunes like "Old Man River," "Lucky Ole' Sun," and "Harbor Lights." Since I did not have a fancy harmonica (chromatic) that had the ability to play sharps and flats, we kept it simple. He seemed to know what ability I had and drew it out of me. I played for Father Ed many times.

On this particular evening, it was approximately 7:30 or 8:00 p.m. when Father Ed dismissed me from my command performance. As I started to walk up the stairway and reach the second landing to the upper floor, something outside caught my eye. In the dimness of the oncoming night, I observed a mass of whiteness in the grassy area just inside the brick and metal fence. The whiteness appeared to be a man sleeping. He was clad in the classic painter's white shirt and pants. He even wore a white cap. He appeared to be about forty years old. Back in those days, everyone believed that people who painted professionally had a drinking problem. It was a hazard of the job. It was expected, at least according to some of the older workers at St. Hedwig. This man was no exception. He appeared to have passed out from overindulging.

I heard voices and wondered where they were coming from. Then I saw her. One of the sisters very carefully walked up to the apparent sleeping individual. She bent over him and kept telling him, "Get up." There was no movement from the man. The nun gently kicked at the sole of his right foot. No response. She kicked a little harder. Nothing. She then delivered a harder kick and did elicit a response from the man. He abruptly sat up and muttered unintelligible gibberish. After focusing on the nun for a few seconds, he readjusted his position on the ground and laid his head down. The nun kicked him again, a little harder, shrieking, "Get up. Get up. You don't belong here."

"Get away from me, lady. Don't bother me" was his reply. The painter rolled over and was going to attempt to sleep once again. At this time, the nun started prodding at his rib and stomach area with a long stick she had picked up from the ground. The painter suddenly sat up, yelled, and swung his arm in her direction. This startled the nun. She screamed and backed away from the prone individual, almost falling down in the process. The stick was dropped. She regained her balance and appeared to hesitate as to what to do next. She was either scared, angry, or both. She walked toward the door just below my view and talked to someone, probably another nun. I could not hear clearly what they were talking about. My window was open, but the noise of the traffic on Harlem Avenue drowned out the particulars. A few minutes later, a group of six or seven older boys, aged fifteen to sixteen, the nun's apparent reinforcements, walked out the door toward the sleeping painter.

This was a rowdy group. I don't know what Sister had told them, but they were ready for action. One of the boys, the obvious leader, yelled at the man on the ground. No response. They all began yelling at the painter to get up. All the kids were yelling at the top of their voices. The original nun walked over to the prone painter who was again stirring and attempting to sit up. She said something to him. Whatever he answered was not what the boys wanted to hear. The biggest boy kicked at the man's upper thigh. It was a strong kick. The man yelled out in pain. Then another boy kicked at him and another and another. Before you knew it, the man was curled up in a fetal position on the ground, pleading for the boys not to hit him. This went on for a good ninety seconds before they stopped. The painter was crying in a low moan. I could see some red blotches, apparent blood, on the all-white clothing. The blood was very noticeable about the shoulders and collar areas. I could not see his hat anywhere. I stood at my vantage point, high above all this activity, just fascinated. I could not believe what I had just witnessed. That man laid very still for the longest time. I could hear an occasional whimper but observed no movement. He appeared to be badly hurt.

Two of the boys grabbed the man's legs in an apparent effort to drag him off the premises. The man must have twitched because both boys dropped his legs simultaneously, almost in a panic. They then began to pummel the man with their fists. They hit him everywhere on his body. All the boys joined in and rained blows on the unfortunate drunk. Suddenly, the activity stopped, and all one could hear were the low, painful moans of the prone individual. The boys backed away from the man and began discussing with the nun what their next step would be.

The nun elected to go to the office and make the telephone call to the police. Most of the boys went back to their dayroom. Two of them "volunteered" to stand guard over their captive. As soon as the nun left, one of the boys kicked the painter in the ribs one last time. This made the man react with a loud "Please, please don't hurt me anymore." This boy then stooped down and picked up what appeared to be a wallet and placed it in his pocket. During a lull in the traffic, I could hear the two older boys talking about the wallet and the money inside. I could barely hear them discussing how they were going to split the money.

I stood on that second floor landing for the longest time. What I witnessed on that summer evening in 1951 or 1952 was an event that I would never forget. I did not think boys of fifteen and sixteen could be so vicious. What happened after the police arrived on the scene further helped to make the incident unforgettable. The two officers parked their police vehicle in the driveway adjacent to the prone individual. The nun who was in charge of the occasion approached the officers and proceeded to tell them what a horrible experience she had because of the painter. One police officer was heard remarking, "Looks like you picked the wrong place to sleep it off, pal." The officer then not so gently helped the drunk into the rear seat of the police car. The man was obviously in a lot of pain, and he let the officer know it. There was no compassion evident from either officer as they drove the wayward painter away from St. Hedwig Orphanage. I hoped that they took him for medical treatment to one of the local hospitals and then home to an anxious wife.

UKULELE LESSONS

It was probably about sixth grade when I got the unenviable opportunity to take some music lessons. I was about eleven or twelve years old when my father presented me with a "special" present: a real, honest-to-goodness ukulele. I think the occasion was my birthday. I don't know where the hell he got the damn thing. It got to the point where I wished I had never laid eyes on it. I may have mentioned to him that it sure would be nice to have a guitar, but a *ukelele*? I had been in this institution for about four years, and all I wanted to do was get out. I was a bit tired of orphanage life. Work, eat, study, play, sleep. Day after day. I needed something to amuse myself. But a ukulele? Geez. No imagination. I think a harmonica would have been better. But my father kept telling me, "It's the same thing as a guitar. Only smaller."

The inevitable happened. My dormitory nun, who shall remain nameless because I forgot her name, ratted on me to the music teacher. Sister Charisima played the piano for all auditorium events. More importantly, she played the organ during church services. She was the expert, of course. When she got word that I was given a legitimate ukulele, not a toy, she took it upon herself to teach me how to play the damn thing. I did not want to learn to play the ukulele.

Now my attitude was not the best. I should have broken the stringed instrument before ever taking that first lesson. Here I was, nine months later, meeting three times a week—Monday, Wednesday, and Friday from 3:00 to 4:00 p.m.—my normal playtime, struggling to make the instrument produce music. The only thing I still remember about the ukulele was how to tune it to the ditty "My Dog Has Fleas." During that hellacious length of time, I reluctantly learned two songs, "My Bonnie Lies over the Ocean" and "Ramona." Keep in mind that all the ukulele was designed for was to produce chords and be accompanied by the human voice. During that period of my life, my voice was beginning to "crack." Not quite the little boy, but not quite the young man either. It was more of a half and half. I still did not want to learn to play this obnoxious instrument. Yet three times a week, I met Sister Charisima in the music room, and we plodded through the lessons. Thank God there were other kids taking piano lessons. The good sister could only devote so much time to me.

Sister Charisima decided that I was ready to make my debut in front of the entire school, well over six hundred kids of varying ages. What did I do to deserve this? My voice, being somewhat unpredictable at this time, would surely fail me. What am I going to do? I fretted and fretted and then came up with a plan. Each time I practiced, I accentuated the cracking voice as much as I could. Sister Charisima, being a legitimate music teacher, could only take so much. After several more weeks of trying to "clear up" my voice, Sister had to admit defeat. She could not get me to steady my shaky voice.

With a very serious look on her face, she summoned me to her desk. She very carefully chose her words and gave me the "devastating" news that it would be wise to discontinue the ukulele lessons at this time. She stated that I would not be performing in front of the student body of St. Hedwig. I had the hardest time pretending that I was hurt and shocked by the turn of events. God, it sure was difficult suppressing my utter joy.

During the next week, the ukulele was accidentally broken by unknown persons who had somehow broken into the music room during the middle of the night. To this day, no one has ever accepted responsibility for that dastardly deed.

UNCLE TONY

There was an older man who used to visit with some of the nuns, usually on the weekend. He was in his sixties, balding, wore glasses, not very tall, with a slight build but always well dressed. He was not affiliated with St. Hedwig Orphanage, but he struck me as being an important person. Occasionally, I would see him surrounded by three or four of the older kids, probably sixteen years of age. I was twelve at this time. It was that awkward time of development, just prior to becoming a real teenager. I used to wonder why these older kids were attracted to Uncle Tony (not his real name). That was even the name the nuns called him. He loved it when the kids referred to him as Uncle Tony. I had heard that he used to give some of the kids money.

One summer weekend, I saw a big 1951 Packard coming up the street at the rear of the gymnasium. This was the area we used as a skating rink. I was skating with my friends when I saw the car and could not believe my eyes. One of the sixteen-year-old kids was actually driving the car. Seated alongside him was Uncle Tony. I had seen that car parked around the orphanage grounds before, and now I knew who it belonged to. It was one beautiful car. White and green. Uncle Tony must have been rich because that was one of the biggest cars I had ever seen. I knew Buicks and Cadillacs, but this one took the cake. That was probably why those older kids hung out with this old man. He let them drive his big car. What a thrill that must be. Suddenly, I wished that I was much older. My dad would never let me drive his car. He kept telling me to wait till I grew up. Hell, I was the second biggest kid in my class at that time. I thought it was time for me to learn how to drive.

A year passed since I saw that Packard being driven by one of St. Hedwig's own. Driving that car was always on my mind. I used to dream about it. I had seen Uncle Tony off and on during the past year, but I never approached him. He always had several of the older kids with him. I think he let every one of them drive his car at one time or another.

I saw the Packard parked by the printshop one Saturday morning. My chores were done, and I stopped by the car to admire it. I was looking inside at the dashboard when a voice startled me. "Pretty, isn't it?" Uncle Tony was speaking to me. There were no other kids around. I was thrilled that I finally got to speak to this man. I wanted to drive his car so bad that it hurt. The next thing he said just floored me. "Do you want to go for a drive?" he asked. I almost ran to the passenger side of the car. As I entered, he asked me my name and how old I was. He even asked me what grade I was in and who my teacher was. I answered all of his questions. I could not take my eyes off the dashboard. It was the plushest I had ever seen. The radio was spectacular. A lot of chrome. The inside matched the outside with the gobs of chrome used in the design. He told me that the Packard had a Hydramatic transmission, and that made it real easy to drive.

I was dying to ask him if I could drive, but I did not dare. I was in heaven just sitting in the front seat. He was treating me like one of the older kids. He let me touch all the knobs and fiddle with the radio. A rich sound came from that radio. I had never heard anything like it before. It must have been state-of-the-art for that time. He drove that Packard past the gymnasium and toward St. Andrew Old Age Home. He made the turn around St. Andrew and brought me back to where he originally picked me up in front of the printshop. He could see how lit up I was. This was just great. As I was starting to get out of the car, he promised me that one of these days, soon, he would let me drive his Packard. He handed me a dollar bill and told me to go get some cigarettes for myself. I profusely thanked him over and over. This guy knew what buttons to push. I was walking on clouds when I snuck off the premises to Mark's Drugstore to buy the cigarettes.

It was about a month later when I spotted Uncle Tony. Two of the older kids were with him, but he quickly dismissed them and beckoned me over. I walked up to him, heart pounding expectantly, wondering if this was the time I would get to drive the car. As promised, Uncle Tony delivered. He told me to get in on the driver's side and handed me the keys to the car. My hands were trembling, but I was able to insert the key into the ignition. Uncle Tony talked me through starting the car and then backing it up to prepare for the drive to St. Andrew, a distance of approximately one mile. I was on top of the world. Ecstatic. I could not believe that this was happening to me. I slowly drove the vehicle at twenty-five miles per hour on the road to St. Andrew, slowing down for the large curve at the end of the gymnasium. Uncle Tony had to tell me to slow down several times because, as he put it, I had a lead foot. I got to the St. Andrew turnaround and carefully guided the Packard back toward St. Hedwig. I was really enjoying this. Uncle Tony kept telling me that I was going to have to visit him when I had some time. He indicated that he lived not far away from St. Hedwig. It was a short bus trip, he had said. I promised him that I would. I would have promised him anything at this point.

The end of the drive came much too quickly. I drove the car into the parking space in front of the printshop, shifted into neutral, and turned the engine off. Uncle Tony told me that I had done an excellent job of driving and that we would have to do it again.

The following Visiting Sunday, I told my dad about driving the Packard. I could not understand his attitude. He was absolutely livid. He told me to never do it again. Maybe he knew something that I didn't.

About a month later, I spotted Uncle Tony's car parked by the infirmary. He apparently was visiting the nuns who worked out of the hospital building. I tried getting over there, but the chores kept piling up. One of the nuns was giving me an extremely hard time and keeping me very busy. My chores would take me to various locations on the premises, and every once in a while, I would spot the Packard, just sitting there. I probably drooled, looking at the car from a distance. I never did catch up to the car or Uncle Tony that day.

Six weeks later, the car showed up at the printshop parking area. I made a beeline toward the printshop, but Uncle Tony was nowhere to be found. I hung around for about an hour when I saw him approaching the car. He seemed to be in a hurry. He dug in his pocket and took out a dollar bill and handed it to me. "Get some cigarettes," he commanded. "When are you going to come and visit me at my place?"

"Pretty soon," I replied.

"How soon?" he asked, sounding irritated.

"How about this weekend, if I can sneak off?" I offered.

We agreed that I would try to make it over to his apartment on Saturday or Sunday but that I should call him prior to doing so. He handed me another dollar bill and told me it was for the telephone calls that I would be making. I thanked him for the money, and he went on his way, driving that big Packard ever so gracefully.

The following Saturday, I got out on Touhy Avenue by crawling under the fence. No one had seen me, and it looked like I had most of the afternoon to myself. I had just eaten lunch. The orphanage administration did not allow us kids off the premises by ourselves, especially thirteen-year-olds, without adult supervision. I knew my way around and knew how to take a bus to just about anywhere in Chicago. I was on my way to Uncle Tony's. With a little bit of luck, he would let me drive his car when I got there. I didn't know what the big deal was about going to his apartment.

He had instructed me to telephone him after I got off the bus, approximately one block from his apartment. I did so, and he gave me directions to his residence. When I arrived, I observed that it was a typical four-story apartment building with about ten apartments on each floor. There was one main door from the street, which allowed one entry into the building. All the hallways were well lighted, and I had no problem finding the correct apartment. His was on the fourth floor.

When I knocked on his door, he opened it immediately. It looked like he had just gotten out of the shower because his hair was wet and he was wrapped in a huge white robe, tied around his waist. He directed me to sit down on the couch and asked if I wanted a soft drink. He brought the drink over and set it on the coffee table. As I looked around the living room, I saw that this was a very small apartment. A bathroom was located just off the kitchen. This one-room apartment had been his home for a number of years. It was just loaded with clutter. Books, pencils, and board games were strewn about. I noted that he had one of those beds that were normally stored within the wall. Peculiarly, his bed was in the down position, taking up most of the living room. It appeared that he was getting ready for bed. At one o'clock in the afternoon?

Then he sat down next to me and started talking to me. I suddenly did not feel very comfortable. Something about this situation disturbed me, but I did not know what it was. I could not help but notice that he had an erection. His robe was no longer tied at the waist. It parted enough to expose his genital area. He saw me staring at his erection.

"Do you want to touch it?" he asked.

"No, no, I don't think so," I stammered.

He said, "Go ahead and touch it. It won't hurt you. You might like it."

I somehow got the courage to stand up. My knees seemed to be having a problem holding me up. They felt like Jell-O.

"I've got to go. I've got to catch the bus before they miss me."

"But you just got here. Don't go," he pleaded. "All you have to do is touch it. I'll give you five bucks if you just touch it. It'll be the easiest five bucks you ever made. If you suck it, I'll give you a double saw ($20). Let me suck you first. There's nothing to be afraid of. No one will know."

He had made his move, and I could not get out of there quick enough. I was never so scared in my life. I hit the apartment door and grabbed the doorknob to open it, but unbeknownst to me, he had turned the dead bolts in the lock position. It wasn't easy, but I somehow managed to clumsily get those dead bolts open and remove my body from the apartment. I ran down the hallway by passing the elevator and took the stairs three or four at a time. By the time I made it out to the street, I was gasping for breath, but I did not slow down. I ran all the way to the bus stop one block away. After a short wait, my bus arrived. I was never so glad to get on a bus. I found a seat at the rear and plopped myself down. I had a lot to think about.

After arriving back at the orphanage, I checked with a few of my friends to make sure I was not missed. I wasn't. I confided in a friend of mine that I had just undergone a weird experience. I did not feel comfortable talking about it, even with my buddy. I did not disclose all the details because I was still shocked that it happened to me. I felt a lot of shame, but I never gave my friend all the facts. Because of the fact that I was absent from the premises without permission made me really wonder if it would have been worth it. Who would believe me? This guy was a friend to a lot of the sisters at St. Hedwig. What adult could I trust anyway? Father Ed? Father Bill? I think that the best way to handle this was to chalk it up to experience and keep my mouth shut.

Uncle Tony did not show his face at St. Hedwig for about a year. Should I have told someone about the incident? What do you suppose would happen if I did say something to one of the nuns or priests? After all, he never did touch me. He only offered me money. Was that enough? Was that against the law? Nevertheless, I steered clear of Uncle Tony for the rest of my tenure at St. Hedwig. I didn't think any adult ever caught on to his game.

THE YOUNG KIDS

When I was thirteen years old, someone, probably my dormitory nun, decided that I was old enough to accept more responsibility. Before I knew what hit me, I found myself being the assistant to the two nuns in charge of the young kids. The young kids consisted of the pre-kindergarten and kindergarten children, boys and girls. Their ages ranged anywhere from two to about four or five. The two nuns in charge of the children were Sister Mary Aquinata and Sister Mary Dulcis. Sister Aquinata, a roly-poly individual with an affable disposition, was in charge of the girls, exclusively, but worked hand in hand with Sister Dulcis. The real boss of the two was Sister Aquinata. Sister Dulcis, the more serious-appearing sister, thinner and taller than Sister Aquinata, and probably younger, was in charge of the boys. I assisted her with her duties in handling the boys. If there was a thirteen-year-old girl who was my apparent counterpart, I was not aware of her. If she existed, then it was part of the master plan not to allow boys and girls to spend any appreciable time together. When I was on duty, she was not. When she was on duty, I must have been elsewhere.

My duties consisted of helping to keep the children in formation when going from one location to another. At mealtimes, I helped serve up the food on their individual plates. They were all capable of eating on their own. I did not have to spoon-feed them. While in the playroom or in the outdoor area reserved for them, my job was to keep them occupied. I kept them busy with games. Yes, I played with them, and they seemed to appreciate it.

At the end of the day, the younger boys were washed clean by Sister Dulcis. She would handle them one at a time. My job was to supervise the rest of the boys, make sure they washed their bodies and brushed their teeth. I had to ensure that they each dutifully dried themselves. Just prior to bedtime, I gave each of the children their allotted daily vitamin. One time I took a vitamin or two, just to see what it felt like. I became so wired that it was difficult for me to sleep for the longest time. I had taken more than I should have.

Generally, after all the boys were ready for bed, Sister Dulcis would dismiss me so that I could visit with my classmates for about an hour. At bedtime, I would dutifully return to the young kid's dormitory and go to sleep in my assigned bed right in their dormitory. Part of my job was to be there, available, if any of the children had a nightmare. This group of children apparently had more than their share of nightmares. Nightmares, or talking in their sleep, seemed to be a daily occurrence. I was constantly being awakened during the night by one of the children. Many times, after the child would be startled awake, they could not remember what it was that was upsetting them. They were then able to go back to sleep without incident. Other times, the same child would be yelling and screaming in their sleep. When I would go to their bedside to attend to them, they would grab on to me and squeeze. They did not want to let go. I suppose that was what a hug was all about. It had been so long that I had experienced a hug that I had forgotten what it was supposed to be. I did not feel especially close to these children. They were the components of a job I was required to do. There was no emotion in the hug that I was giving them. Apparently, it worked for them though. It usually settled them down for a good night's sleep.

Upon arising, it fell upon me to supervise the young lads in getting ready for the day. They had to be dressed, wash their faces, and brush their teeth so that they could line up in column of twos and march off to the dining room for breakfast. One of the perks of this job was that I did not have to attend daily church services. The young kids were usually finishing up their food in the dining hall when church let out and the rest of the population entered for breakfast.

This job only lasted for the summer, but it took its toll. I probably gained thirty pounds. The young kids did not receive the typical orphanage fare. They had a special cook who prepared their meals. The same person who prepared the workers' meals was the one who prepared the meals for the youngsters. To put it bluntly, the food given the young kids was outstanding. Of course, I got to eat my share, and then some. Hence, the extra weight.

Summer came to a close, and I was glad to get back into the routine with my own classmates. Most of them thought that I had been punished when given the job of helping to take care of the young kids. Maybe I was, but I look upon it as a good experience. I learned a thing or two, and I also made some points with the administration of St. Hedwig. You never knew when those points would come in handy.

FIRE

It was about two o'clock in the afternoon on a Sunday. We were enjoying some nice spring weather in preparation for the upcoming Easter holiday. Several of us were swinging on the wooden glider when we saw the smoke coming out of the sewing room on the top floor of our building. Simultaneously we could faintly hear sirens in the distance. The Niles Fire Department was only a block away, but the orphanage was actually within the Chicago city limits. Or was it? It was situated right on the border. Who would respond? To this day, I do not know which fire department handled that fire.

As more of the kids became aware of the fiery impending disaster, they began to crowd around the open area between the dining room and the main building. That's when I noticed that some of the nuns from the girls' side had brought their wards to see firsthand what was going on. After all, when fire trucks entered off Touhy Avenue with sirens blaring and red lights flashing, it will get one's attention. Something was happening on the boys' side of St. Hedwig, and every one wanted to witness the event. The fact that it was the dreaded sewing room that was on fire helped stir up interest. The sewing room was occasionally used as a punishment location for errant boys and girls. Many of us had experienced a strap or wooden paddle on our bottoms while being detained in this torture chamber.

About this time, we saw the fire trucks pulling up and parking in strategic locations in the open area. As the crowd moved back, the firemen jumped down from their vehicles and removed hoses and axes from the fire truck. All of us kids were in awe as the firemen went about their duties. Six firemen went charging through the main door on the first floor for the long trek up the stairs to the top floor. There were no elevators in this building. That's when we saw the hook and ladder truck come rolling up. The driver of the hook and ladder positioned the truck so that the ladder could be extended to the top floor. It seemed to take forever for them to get the ladder moving toward the top of the building.

The firemen inside the building appeared to be having a tough time getting the hose to the top floor. By now, the sewing room was completely ablaze. Fire was coming out of all three windows. The billowing black smoke swirled straight up into the sky. What a sight this was. I was standing toward the front of the crowd of students with several of my friends, observing the fire. I made a remark to them that I wished the whole building would go up in flames. I thought only my friends had heard me, but I was wrong. When I began to sing a song about burn, burn, burn, I felt the back of my head being struck by what I thought was a baseball bat. It turned out to be the hand or fist of one of my "favorite" nuns. I went to the floor in a heap. I was so stunned I could not hear or see anything for about a minute. I could then hear my friends snickering about the incident. No moral support from my friends. Apparently, the nun who struck me had left to attend to some other errant kids who also were making fun of the situation. After being helped to my feet by my friends, we continued to watch the firemen do their job.

Suddenly there were no flames. I saw eight or nine firemen appear on the roof, heavily engrossed in whatever it was they do after a fire. I was wondering where they came from when it dawned on me that most of the fire trucks entered the orphanage premises on the Harlem Avenue side adjacent to the main office, out of our line of sight. Several of the firemen were chopping away at sections of the roof with their axes. They continued their mop-up operation for several hours. A rumor went through the crowd that defective wiring was the probable cause of the blaze.

The sewing room was completely gutted. It took months and months to get rid of the acrid smoke odor from the four-story building.

It also took every bit of the time to rebuild the sewing room. Out of the ashes came a blessing. Was it coincidence or not? I personally do not recall the infamous sewing room being used as a punishment room ever again.

THE SPELLING BEE

Sr. Mary Leonette Schwientek was my seventh-grade teacher. Although I continued to excel academically, Sister Leonette noticed another of my talents that she wanted to enhance: spelling.

Sometime during the fall of 1952, St. Hedwig Orphanage experienced more than their share of spelling bees. Spelling always came easy for me. More often than not, I was the last person standing. It used to excite me when older grades were involved and I would still be the last speller standing. The students of St. Hedwig were being groomed for involvement in legitimate spelling bees using the same methods in area, district, state, and national bees.

My teacher must have really liked me because she even arranged for a tutor to help me out with the more difficult and foreign words. The tutor turned out to be Russ Lukes, my best friend. The two of us were afforded privileges because of our involvement in the spelling program. This all paid off, especially in the eyes of the sisters, when I won the local district championship of Chicago. The event took place somewhere on the north side of Chicago, necessitating the assistance of my dad to get us there. Even though my dad lived on the south side of Chicago, he readily agreed to chauffeur my teacher Sister Leonette and I to whatever school was hosting the event.

The spelling bee took place in a small auditorium, which was attended by approximately fifty adults. There were about twenty-five participants about the age of twelve or thirteen, representing as many schools, who were actively participating in the contest. I was the only one representing an orphanage. When I was introduced, I got some strange looks from people, but I was already used to that. Each participant must have had an entourage of family with them. How wonderful. I, at least, had my dad and my teacher.

I was very nervous. A lot of people and a lot of competition. The folding chairs we sat on were not comfortable. That did not help matters. In fact, all the kids seemed nervous except one. He was a bespectacled thirteen-year-old from one of the bigger public schools. He had pure genius written all over him. I figured him as my stiffest competition. Other kids that I had zeroed in on did not appear to represent a threat. One kid in particular looked like he did not want to be there. He was probably forced into it by his parents or his teacher. I was brimming with confidence even though I was a bit shaky. With a little luck and a prayer or two, I saw no reason I could not win this spelling bee. In fact, it was pointed out to me by more than one of the sisters that all the students at St. Hedwig had said prayers on my behalf for this event. I had better win. A lot of people were rooting for me. If I did not win, I would never hear the end of it.

The first casualty of the afternoon was "the genius." He slipped up on what I thought was one of the easier words. Others fell along with him. For what it was worth, I could have correctly spelled any of those words.

After the nervousness wore off, I blew them away. The administrators of the spelling bee, members of the board of education no doubt, must have used the same book to select their words for the spelling bee that Russ and I had used for our studies. It came down to three finalists—a girl of about thirteen, the guy who did not want to be there, and me. But they too met their match. First, the boy faltered. Then it was the girl's turn. The hardest word that was given to me, and it was the final word, was silhouette.

Once again, I was the last one standing and the apparent winner. My teacher, Sister Leonette, was beaming. You could not remove that grin of hers. I had truly made her day. My father did not realize how much this meant to me. All he wanted to do was get Sister

Leonette and me into his car for the trip back to St. Hedwig. That was understandable because he had a long drive back to the south side of Chicago to a neighborhood called West Pullman. It would take him nearly an hour to get home after dropping us off at the orphanage. I felt sorry for him. He looked so tired. I did not give it another thought though and thoroughly enjoyed the moment. I felt like a movie star. I shook hands with just about everyone in the auditorium before we went to the car. Everyone knew who I was and what I had accomplished. I was walking on air and feeling really good about myself.

After dropping us off at St. Hedwig and the obligatory cup of coffee for my dad, he finally left for his trip home. Word had preceded my entrance into the gymnasium, and I was swarmed by my friends and classmates when I entered. Russ took the opportunity to remind me that I could not have done it without him. But he was proud of me, I could tell.

Sister Leonette had informed me that I had won the district championship of that area and that I would be appearing in another spelling bee at the next level. As near as I could figure, it was to be for the championship of the Chicago area. The neat thing about it was that the event was going to be televised. Wow! I was going to be on TV. All the kids at St. Hedwig were going to witness the event. I was enjoying my celebrity status more and more.

It must have been about a month later when the big event was just around the corner. Sister Leonette had arranged for Russ and me to be "patients" at the infirmary where we could study without distractions and interruptions. Russ was a good tutor, and we did study. We probably spent two days at the infirmary going over all the spelling books. I was as ready as I could be. Russ pronounced me fit for my appearance on television.

The big day came, and suddenly I found myself and Sister Leonette being driven by one of the priests to a television studio somewhere in downtown Chicago. I don't know what happened to my father. He probably had to work. When we arrived at the studio, we were ushered into a large room loaded with kids my own age. There must have been fifty of them. They all seemed to have both of their parents with them. I, at least, had my two guardians. For some reason though, I was not feeling as confident as I was accustomed to. Nevertheless, I was as ready as I was ever going to be. These kids were probably about the same age as me, but they all appeared to be much older.

A youngish man in his late twenties wearing a black suit, white shirt, and black tie began to speak to the throng. A hush fell over the group as we all struggled to hear what he had to say. "Be relaxed and as comfortable as possible" is all I can remember. It was probably good advice. But the best advice came when he reminded everyone to "hit the bathrooms" before entering the studio area.

All fifty of us were shown to a large studio. There were approximately six rows of seats encircling half the room. All the seats looked down on a stage area where the announcer would be standing. I felt like I was a United Nations delegate due to the seating arrangement. On the desk in front of each place, there was a pad of paper and a special pen honoring the event. We were told that the pen was ours to keep. It was a nice black pen with gold lettering. Then I saw the television cameras. There must have been three or four of them. Someone explained that the only way you could tell if you were being televised was when the red light came on and the camera was pointed at you. One of the technicians explained that millions of people would be watching the program and that it was normal to be nervous. Nervous? You could just feel it. Many of us had this look of concern on our faces. Millions of people. Wow! Yep, I was definitely nervous, but I was ready. Let's get this show on the road.

When the spelling bee started, it took no time for the first casualty. Then the next. And the next. I recall that I made it through two rounds and was able to correctly spell my given words. On the third round, the word given to me was "admissible." I had spelled that word for Russ many times, but for some reason, I spelled it as a-d-m-i-s-s-a-b-l-e. That was it. My short life as a television star was suddenly and rudely over.

When I got back to St. Hedwig, I was no longer treated like a celebrity. I was allowed to melt into the herd and go back to normal. It was a wild ride while it lasted. Months later, I would hear an occasional compliment from other kids about my television appearance. One of them told me that I did not look like me even though he knew it was me because "Sister said so." A couple of the older girls really took a liking to me ever since that event. Prior to the spelling bee, they would not have given me the time of day. I did enjoy the perks. Wait till next year.

MR. COCKY

It was hard to believe that it was a year ago since I had appeared on television after winning the district championship of Chicago. It was September 1953, the start of the new school year. My teachers were once again grooming me for another run at the spelling championships. I was game. I was ready to go. The preliminary bee for my area was to take place in October, hardly a month away. I was looking forward to it.

During the year, I had many ups and downs. Initially, the kids at the school, specifically my classmates, treated me like a celebrity. I just loved the attention. Even some of the nuns treated me in a special way. But somewhere along the line, that treatment began to diminish. I did not give it much thought, but I would occasionally wonder why their attitude toward me changed.

Russ, my longtime friend, was once again my tutor. He tutored me two or three times a week during the evening hours. He also tutored me during regular class hours after our assignments were completed. During one of our sessions, we found the teacher's stash of hard "Christmas candy" hidden in a closet. We helped ourselves to the candy to the point that we both became sick. To this day, I never touch the stuff. I took that as one of life's lessons to leave that stuff alone. Russ never did learn.

During an exceptionally long tutorial session, I asked Russ why so many of my classmates were avoiding me.

He turned to me with a look of shock. "You really want to know?" There was a long pause, and then he answered. "You've become a big jerk," he responded.

"Who, me? How? What are you talking about?" I retorted.

"Mike, you have let a little success get to your head. You have become cocky. In fact, you are the cockiest person I know."

I know that I argued with Russ for some time over that issue. Finally, he assured me that we were still friends and would continue to be friends. He really knocked the wind out of my sails, but unfortunately, it was short-lived.

A few days later, St. Hedwig Orphanage had their official second annual spelling bee. Once again, I was the last person standing. Just for drill, my teacher, Sister Mary Alexia, arranged for several of the brighter high school kids to participate in the contest. I guess my eighth-grade head really swelled up at this point. I was probably impossible to live with. My friends continued to shun me. Russ tolerated me.

The day for the preliminary spelling bee arrived. Once again, it was being held at a school on the north side of Chicago. My father was again asked to be the chauffeur to which he readily agreed. Russ even agreed to accompany us to the spelling bee. When we arrived at the small auditorium, it was like watching a rerun on television. I found out years later that I did not walk into that auditorium. I swaggered in, like the conquering hero of the previous year. That body language must have turned off a lot of the audience, but it went clear over my head.

The proctor was explaining the rules of the contest while I was thinking to myself how I was going to win. I was going to blow them away. Just like last year. Suddenly, it was showtime. The first three or four kids were able to spell their words. When it got to me, the proctor gave me the word "elephant." Hell, I knew that word. I could spell it backward if I had to. Then I spelled it: e-l-a-p-h-a-n-t.

"Wait. That's wrong," I stammered.

"Too late," said the proctor. "You know the rules."

Did he have a gleam in his eye? I thought to myself. I almost thought I heard a muffled cheer from the audience, but I am sure it was all in my fat head. I sadly got up from my chair and walked out of the building. The swagger was lost, hopefully, forever. I have never held my head as low as I did when I walked out of that auditorium.

When I got back to St. Hedwig, I was not treated very well. The kids in the lower grades took great glee in laughing at my fallen stature. I was no longer someone to look up to. My peers snickered a lot. In fact, they were relentless. They never let me forget my unruly behavior. And I did not blame them. I had just learned what the definition of humility was. I was experiencing it. My teacher even took great relish in placing me on my knees, in class, for the remainder of the school week. It was not pleasant, but I knew I had to handle the punishment with grace if I was to keep any of my dignity at all. It took a long while but my classmates finally allowed me back into their circle. Peer pressure can be a wonderful thing in the right place.

Many years later, when Russ and I renewed our friendship after a long lapse, he asked me if I was still cocky. It took a moment or two for it to sink in. We then both burst out laughing.

ROLL OUT THE BARREL

Someone had left a fifty-five-gallon detergent barrel at the ash pile. The ash pile was located between the barn and garbage can building. In those days, much of the trash was burned on the ash pile. Usually there was a smoldering fire going. Paper, rags—you name it, we burn it. There was a large brick incinerator complete with a brick chimney, which was in constant use. Regular garbage, such as foodstuffs, was placed in thirty-gallon metal cans located in the garbage can building. There were about twelve cans in that location. Shortly after the garbage trucks would pick up the garbage, I would have to take fresh garbage and dump it in that building. That's when I discovered where flies come from. The bottoms of most of the cans were loaded with white maggots. I hated the chore of having to dump the garbage.

The fifty-five-gallon drum fascinated us. Eddie and Richard quickly grabbed it and headed for the hill located by the barn. I watched as each of them took turns rolling down the hill while inside it. It looked like a lot of fun. I wanted to have my turn. None of us gave a thought to the danger that was involved. The can could easily roll toward the smoldering fire not very far away. A vehicle traveling in the vicinity could easily strike the occupied barrel. The dizzying effect did not seem to bother anyone.

Ronnie came up to join us in our adventure. Russ was not far behind. We spent most of the afternoon rolling one another down the hill without incident. When Russ took his third turn, I was the one to help propel him down the hill. I started the barrel rolling, but this time, I stayed with it a bit longer. I was going to make sure he got the ride of his life. Then it happened. I slipped and fell, catching my elbow on the rim of the barrel. This opened up a gash about one inch long. A lot of blood came from the wound. I was aware of Russ at the bottom of the hill, attempting to make his way up to my location. He was still dizzy from the ride of his life. That's when George, an adult worker, saw what was going on. He immediately took his clean hankie and made a tourniquet on my arm to slow down the flow of blood. He then immediately started walking me toward the infirmary building, which was located about 150 yards away. The nun at the infirmary, Sister Teresita, was a registered nurse and would be able to help me. She saw me and my entourage approaching.

By now, the blood was slowing down a bit, probably due to the tourniquet. Sister Teresita went to work immediately. She indicated that it probably needed stitches, but she would put a special dressing on it to help the cut heal properly. No stitches were used, much to my relief. She cleaned and cleaned the cut with a special ointment. Then she did her magic and put on the special dressing. I distinctly recall that the cut hurt like hell. No tears from this tough guy, at least not in front of my buddies.

I had to return to the infirmary numerous times over the next two weeks for a dressing change. After all the smoke had cleared and I examined the wound, I was astonished at the size of the cut and how well it had healed. Even though the scar is not as distinct as it was then, I still occasionally check it out and fondly remember the good times.

EIGHTH-GRADE GRADUATION

It was April 1954, and graduation from eighth grade was on the horizon. At this point in time, I had been in St. Hedwig Orphanage for close to six full years. This was to be the most exciting and defining moment of my stay in this "prison."

Graduating from the eighth grade was the biggest deal that could happen to a St. Hedwig inmate. Once you got out of the eighth grade, you became one of the "big guys." St. Hedwig offered only the freshman and sophomore years of high school. If you wanted to continue your schooling, you were sent to Holy Trinity High School on the north side of Chicago. The girls were sent to Good Counsel, also on the north side, to finish high school. However, if you dropped out of school after your sophomore year, you became a "worker" for the orphanage administration. Naturally, the nuns encouraged more schooling. I myself was looking forward to attending Holy Trinity if I was still going to be stuck here. You were really someone important when you got to attend high school on the "outside." The only two guys I vividly remember going to Holy Trinity High School were Frank and Fred Stopka, twin brothers. They even got to play on the football team.

Right now, my eighth-grade class, especially the guys, wanted our graduation to be something that no one would ever forget. Keep in mind that we had very limited funding available for this event.

Those of us who had a parent or family would probably have an easier time of it. Then again, maybe not.

The rage at that time was Levi's and white T-shirts. Of course, that would never go for a graduation ceremony. Also popular were powder blue suits, pink "Mr. B" shirts, and knitted black boxer-type ties. Boxer shoes were also in vogue, especially the blue suede variety. Some singer made the shoes really popular. The conspiracy was set. All of us guys were going to do all in our power to attire ourselves in the latest fashion. Oh, I almost forgot, the pants had to be "pegged."

I had one hell of a time convincing my dad that I needed a powder blue suit for graduation. He wanted to get the traditional navy blue suit. I remained steadfast on this one, and he finally relented. I wasn't about to push my luck for a pink shirt or a knitted black tie. I did not even ask for the boxer shoes. I had a little money saved up, and I intended to use some of it. This ceremony was becoming more and more important to me as the June date got closer. My dad came through though. He took me out one Saturday to a men's store. I believe it was Morris B. Sachs. They had a powder blue suit in stock, and luckily, it was my size. The tie I was able to remove from a display rack at the men's store without anyone spotting me. The shirt is a story in itself.

I had a white dress shirt that was given to me for Christmas by my dad. It fit well and had a "Mr. B" collar, but it was not pink. I went to our local dime store (remember Kresge's on Touhy Avenue?) and bought a pink dye kit. I forget the brand name, but it was the only brand that carried the color pink. I read the directions and prepared to dye my beautiful white shirt. I filled up a one gallon bucket with cold water (per the instructions) and mixed in the dye pack. Ooh, that water did turn pink. Wow! Hope the shirt turns out as well. I almost cringed when I placed my beautiful white dress shirt in that bucket. The instructions said to leave it in there, undisturbed, for four hours. I think the small print said something about a much larger container for that gallon of liquid.

After the four hours were up, I rushed over to where I had the bucket stashed. With great anticipation, I lifted the now bright pink shirt out of the one-gallon bucket and squeezed the excess water from the garment. Then I unfurled the shirt and snapped it in the air like cracking a whip to get rid of excess water and dye. When I hung it up on a wooden pole to dry, I discovered that the pink in the shirt was not a solid pink. I believe I was supposed to swirl the shirt around in the much larger container than I used. The net result was one ruined white-with-multiple-shades-of-pink dress shirt. I had probably discovered the secret of tie-dyeing years before its time. This expensive disaster was beginning to annoy me.

So what do I do about a new pink "Mr. B." dress shirt? And then there are the shoes: blue suede shoes, no less. This graduation was turning out to be an expensive event in my life. I hope it's worth it. I received special permission from Father Ed to go shopping one Saturday morning. The first store I entered had quite a display of shirts. There were no "Mr. B's" in sight. The second store seemed a bit pricey for a thirteen-year-old kid from an orphanage. I asked about prices anyway. They wanted a minimum of $30 for a pink "Mr. B." That was more than my dad paid for my suit. The third store I checked out had countless "Mr. B" shirts. However, the clerks failed to notice an about-to-graduate-from-grammar-school teenager. After wasting about fifteen minutes, I walked out of the store. This venture was turning into another disaster.

In the very next store I entered, I found what I was looking for. The price was reasonable, and the shirt required french cuff links. That was great because I had a set of cuff links that I had never been able to use. I couldn't even remember where I got them. Probably from a five-and-dime. I don't recall paying for them. Nevertheless, my shirt problems were over.

The first week of June was approaching, and I still had not gotten my shoes. It seems that all the parents and family were against the blue suede shoes. My dad used to take me to Maxwell Street near downtown, south side area, and never paid more than $5 for a pair of shoes. The cheapest price I could find for blue suede boxer shoes was $35. I probably checked out ten million shoe stores before I finally found what I was looking for. Ten dollars was a lot of money in those days, and to spend that on a pair of shoes was crazy. Like I said, I hoped this graduation would be worth it. My life savings were tied up in those shoes. What's really crazy is that I had to hide them until graduation day. If my dad got wind that I had bought those shoes, who knows what he would have done. He wasn't much of a disciplinarian, but still, why push him? The first time he laid eyes on those shoes was at my graduation ceremony. I was one of the few guys wearing blue suede shoes. I was SOMEBODY!

My dad never did say a word about my boxer shoes. I paid double what he had ever paid for a pair of my shoes. When he asked about my beautiful white dress shirt, I told him it got lost in the laundry. And as far as this graduation being the most momentous event in my young life, yeah, it probably was.

If you were to take a good look at my 1954 graduation picture, there were only three navy blue suits, one dark gray, one white, and the rest powder blue. One of the boys wore a bow tie. Nine of us, on the other hand, wore knitted black boxer-type ties. An interesting side note to that graduation picture: out of twenty-two boys posing for the picture, nine of them had no hint of a smile. Of course, the nine of us nonsmilers had prearranged that. All seven girls wore pink dresses with black belts and smiles.

PRIVILEGES AND RESPONSIBILITIES

During most of my tenure at St. Hedwig Orphanage, I dealt with the high school principal, Sister Mary Edith. She was a tall, husky nun. Mean looking. My relationship with her was never good. She had dining room duty when I met her on that first month. She was in charge of getting certain chores done. I got to know her very well as she stood over my sister Sandra while we were eating supper one day. Unfortunately, we were having chicken gizzards as the main course. Sandra could not tolerate chicken gizzards. Never could. Sister Edith happened to watch as my sister handed me the chicken gizzards off her plate.

"No! No! No!" she hollered. "Put that meat back on her plate!" she directed to me. I had no choice. She was in charge. My sister was becoming upset with the turn of events. Then she started to cry. I hated it when Sandra cried. That was when I experienced helplessness the most, and it was not a pleasant feeling. I had generally been able to help my sister in instances like this. I did not think Sister Edith had any business dealing with kids our age.

My sister and I sat in that dining room for more than an hour. Everyone else had finished eating and had left. The only ones left were the kids cleaning up. Sister Edith never left our area until she walked toward the front of the dining room to confer with "Grumpy," Sister Florentine. I put the offending chicken gizzards in my mouth and chewed them as fast as I could. I am sure that at least one of them went down my throat whole. She got back to the table and saw that the gizzards were gone. She naively told my sister that she took a while but that she did a good job at finishing her plate. Or did Sister Edith just get tired of making sure we did the "right" thing? She reminded us that there were people starving all over the world and that St. Hedwig students were expected to clean off their plates.

As I got older, my dealings with Sister Edith became more frequent. I firmly believe that she was the inventor of whitewash, that water-soluble paint that was used outside to keep things white. There were many rocks and boulders within the confines of the orphanage. They were always a gleaming white color. My buddy Russ Lukes and I were responsible for keeping them that way. Whitewash paint kept those rocks looking good. It seemed that the two of us were always in trouble. But a lot of the chores I had to do alone. Maybe I got into trouble more than he did. One other summertime chore I always seemed to get stuck with was leveling the weeds close to the fence along Touhy Avenue near Gorky Hill. If I had a decent tool to deal with the weeds, I would not have minded so much. I had to use a hand scythe. That weedy area must have run a good 150 feet. It took forever and ever to complete the task properly. This was done usually in the heat of the day. I was expected to cut back the weeds at least five feet from the fence. Never did I ever have a partner for that chore. As I recall, under the best of circumstances, it took the better part of three days to complete. God, how I hated Sister Edith.

About the time I graduated from eighth grade, there was a sudden change in high school teachers. Overnight, Sister Edith seemed to have disappeared. She was replaced by Sister Mary Marcy. Sister Marcy was the direct opposite of Sister Edith. She was shorter and thinner, soft-spoken, and always seemed to have a smile.

Russ and I were up to the new challenge. We never could get away much with Sister Edith. We were going to test this new nun immediately and see how we fared. She seemed to be a pushover. Boy, were we in for a surprise.

Sister Marcy summoned Russ and I to one of the classrooms and introduced herself to us. She proceeded to give us a pep talk. I know that I probably had a smirk on my face and almost started laughing. Russ elbowed me *hard* when Sister Marcy was not looking.

I behaved and listened to her little speech. She talked about duties and responsibilities and privileges. I had heard it all before and did not think there was going to be anything new going on. When she finished up with us, she gave us permission to leave the premises and go outside the gates of the orphanage to get ourselves some ice cream. This was a very rare treat. In fact, it was her treat. She gave us the money, which amounted to about 25¢ each.

I couldn't believe it. Russ couldn't believe it. We walked toward the Tastee Freeze located within the shadows of the orphanage buildings on Harlem Avenue, but across the street and away from any meddling nuns. We were stunned by our stroke of good luck. If this is what she meant by privileges, then it looked like we were going to have a fine relationship. However, we would find out about the additional duties and responsibilities soon enough.

Without realizing what was happening to us, Russ and I found out that we were being groomed for the top positions on the student council. This was a new concept that seemed to be catching on in schools in the Chicago area and probably across the country. After a field trip to the Chicago City Council and sitting in on one of their meetings, the campaign started. We found ourselves giving speeches to the freshmen and sophomore classes. The enthusiasm was incredible. I really got into the role of candidate in a big way. So did Russ. He was a good public speaker. There were also speeches in front of the entire school at the assembly hall. It was exciting.

The day of voting finally came. Russ received more votes than I did and was elected president of the student council. I was right behind him with the second most number of votes and was elected vice president and treasurer. Ronald Weiss was elected to the office of secretary, and Frank Lewandowski was elected sergeant-at-arms.

As the months went on, all of the high school kids were given more privileges than was thought possible. Especially Russ and me. But we found out that we were a lot busier than we had ever been. Sister Marcy had us supervising work details constantly. We were enjoying our newly found responsibilities. We felt good about life in general. Our underclassmen treated us with new respect. What was going on? Sister Marcy was a genius. She latched on to the two biggest potential troublemakers in the school and transformed them into productive members of the student council. I guess it was some sort of divine intervention. On the other hand, Sister Marcy became one of the most respected teachers that I ever had. I really believe that she turned my life around and that of my friend Russ.

The student court was another of Sister Marcy's innovations. As the vice president of the student council, I sat as the presiding judge over numerous cases of mischief and disrespect toward the sisters. The ages of the students appearing before the court were from seven to fourteen. I do not recall ever having to pass judgment on one of my peers. I was about fifteen at the time. Sister Marcy made sure that I had a list of chores for the various offenders. She sat in on all sessions to ensure I did the right thing. One of the nuns would make the formal accusation in court. Interestingly, the accused would not deny that it occurred. It was not a matter of guilt or innocence but what punishment would fit the infraction. Sassing back to a nun was considered a serious offense. Extra chores usually took care of the unruly child. A nun's accusation did carry a lot of weight.

Believe it or not, this procedure was run like a well-oiled machine. I could not have abused my power if I had tried. Under Sister Marcy's tutelage, the student court of St. Hedwig was successful. Punishment for an infraction was more readily accepted by the students, especially when it came from an older student.

There were many things I learned from this experience. It taught me to be less judgmental of others as well as to listen to both sides of a story before drawing a conclusion. I also learned not to act in haste. The one thing that really jumps out at me that I learned from these experiences is not to lose one's temper. Stay in control of your emotions at all times. These lessons have followed me throughout my life and have helped make me the person that I am today. God bless Sister Marcy.

MY FIRST BEER

Russ and I were finally dismissed by Sister Mary Canisia, the boy's dining room nun, and were getting ready to exit the dining hall. It had been raining all morning. It finally appeared that the rain was going to let up and allow us to play some baseball this afternoon. Sister Canisia had really put us through the paces. Russ and I had been in trouble again and were doing extra duty working for her. It could have been worse. At least she liked us.

She yelled at us when it was appropriate because we were always doing something wrong. But we had such an effect on her that she was suspicious of us when she just thought we were thinking of doing something wrong. She had our number, and we knew it. Anyway, my good buddy and I had to mop the entire boys' side of the dining hall. This took us about two hours, and we were glad to be done.

As we walked out the dining room door, we paused in the doorway to figure out our next move. It was still too wet to play baseball, and we had several hours to kill before we had to return to the dining hall for supper. Then I saw it. A case of Blatz Beer cans, sitting on a windowsill of one of the adult workers. Above the laundry room, directly across from the dining hall, the workers' quarters took up the entire second story of the building. The back side of the workers' quarters faced toward the dining hall. Each room had a window facing the dining room area. The window could easily be reached with an extension ladder, if necessary. We walked toward the window, which held the beer. It was not more than fifteen feet from our location. I pointed up toward the window.

"Do you see it?" I asked Russ.

"See what?"

"The beer, dummy."

"Oh," Russ responded.

"Oh! All you can say is 'oh'?" I shot back.

Now I knew neither of us ever had a beer since we had known each other. We may have sampled a beer prior to St. Hedwig, but that was so long ago it did not count. We were both fifteen years old and full of adventure. We had to get that beer down from the window, but how? The cardboard case was soaked from all the rain we had earlier, and one of the beers had fallen to the ground in the flood control area at the base of the building. The rest of the beer was just waiting for us to retrieve. I thought we would try to find a transom stick and take our chances in knocking the beer down. I knew there was one in the dining hall. The transom stick was about five feet long, and if one stood on the railing below the window, the beer could possibly be touched with the transom stick. Then again, maybe not. However, Russ suggested that we throw rocks and whatever else we could heave toward the case of beer. Who knows, a well-placed throw could dislodge some of the beer. This was profound thinking for a fifteen-year-old.

Both of us had our baseball gloves with us. One of us always had a baseball on hand. Would you believe Russ and I spent the better part of the hour tossing rocks, pieces of two-by-four lumber, and, finally, the baseball at the case of beer in hopes of dislodging the cans. Russ tossed the ball, hitting the window first and bouncing off the case. This seemed to cause movement within the case of beer. In the meantime, I had retrieved the one can that had fallen to the ground. I hid it in the bushes while we were busy trying to get another beer, at least. Finally, after a concerted joint effort of tossing and tossing the baseball and striking the case of beer in various spots without breaking the window, the soaked cardboard finally gave way and allowed four beers to fall to the ground.

We were really proud of ourselves, Russ and I. We gathered up our five beers and proceeded to the "ash pile." The "ash pile" was the local dump, the location where garbage to be burned was placed. Not too many people came around there, so we were assured of some privacy. Upon arriving at the "ash pile," Russ asked me how we were going to get the beer open. I hadn't really given it any thought. "We'll think of something," I answered him.

We explored the "ash pile" for a tool of some kind. Or a piece of sharp metal. Maybe a nail or a screwdriver. Anything that would open the beer. We had come this close, and yet we were so far from opening the beer cans. There were no pull tabs in those days. In the meantime, one of our classmates, Joe Plachy, had come by. He worked in the chicken coop area by the farm adjacent to the "ash pile." We told him of our plight. He disappeared around the corner and headed toward the barn, a brick building located about one hundred feet from our location. We watched him from a distance as he reached into his pocket and removed a ring of keys. He used one of the keys to open the door of the barn, entered, and then exited with a flat-edged shovel in his hand. He then began to walk toward us.

What was he thinking? How was he going to open our beer with a spade? He solemnly walked up to us, took one of the beers, placed it upright on the ground, raised the shovel with one hand, and carefully struck the beer can with a corner of the tool. Presto! It did the trick, even though we lost half of the beer spewing out from the blow. I took the shovel from Joe, grabbed my own beer, and tried to make my hole. After several attempts, Joe took the shovel from me, took the beer, lined it up on the ground, and struck the beer with the corner, again spewing half the contents on the ground. Hell, half a beer is better than none. We repeated the process with the other cans of beer, completely ruining one of the cans with an ill-placed blow, nearly cutting the can in half. All of the contents disappeared from that can all over the ground. Russ, Joe, and I enjoyed our first beer.

We had beer on our clothing and on our faces, but that did not take the fun out of enjoying a beer. Although the beer was warm, neither of us would admit that it tasted horrible. Although there weren't enough beer to get us tipsy, we convinced one another that it was one of life's great experiences.

While eating supper in the dining hall, one of the nuns had walked by my table and remarked to no one in particular, "Someone smells like they fell into a can of beer." If she only knew. Nothing else was said, so I continued to eat my meat loaf and potatoes as if nothing mattered.

BOURBON, ANYONE?

It was Christmas Eve 1954. In a couple of days, I was going to turn fifteen years old. That meant that I had spent more than half of my life in this terrible place. I was eight when I was introduced to orphanage life. Don't get me wrong. St. Hedwig wasn't all that bad. But there were certainly a lot of ups and downs. I wanted out. I had no concept of what life would be outside the confines of the orphanage. I wanted to live with a mother and a father like normal people. In this place, everything was structured. Day to day. Week to week. Month to month. Hell, you could plan a year in advance and know exactly what was going to occur on each day.

Monday, breakfast always consisted of cereal, usually cornflakes. It was about this time that Frosted Flakes and Corn Pops made their debut on the American market. Yes, we did get our share of the new cereals. Tuesday was always toast, except when the toaster was broken. Wednesday was a crapshoot. Sometimes plain old bread with peanut butter or lard. Lard was not as bad as it sounds. It had tiny black bits of meat debris, which made it quite tasty. Thursday breakfast usually consisted of a coffee-cake-type homemade sweetbread. Friday was special "orphan buns," a crisp, kaiser roll type of bread, which tasted outstanding with butter. It was delivered in large paper bags to the orphanage bakery personnel. I recall specifically walking around the boys' dining room with a bag of the rolls, doling them out to each table before breakfast was served. Saturday was donations day. The local bakeries would donate their leftovers and items that did not sell during the week. I really can't recall what was served for Sunday breakfast. We did get our share of oatmeal and farina, though not on a regular basis. Every day, each table was graced with a pitcher of milk and a pitcher of coffee already mixed with milk and sugar. They had you drinking coffee, albeit with milk and sugar, from about the third grade. I won't even talk about our lunches and suppers. We knew months ahead of time what was going to be served.

One thing I specifically recall was that on Friday, the pork chops for the Saturday or Sunday meal were fried. They chose Friday because in those days, it was a no-meat day for the Catholics. In fact, it was a mortal sin for a Catholic to eat meat on a Friday. Those freshly fried pork chops sure did look good. By the time they were served to us on Saturday or Sunday, they were a bit dried out. The large ovens did an adequate job of warming the meat. All I can say is that freshly fried pork chops tasted the best when eaten on Friday. I could not fathom what the nuns would have done to me if they caught me eating meat on Friday.

During the summer, we would get bananas shipped by the crate. Bananas do not keep well and will rot quickly. The good sisters consistently dreamed up new recipes to efficiently use up the bananas. Sliced bananas with milk and sugar was one of my favorites. Sliced bananas sprinkled with orange juice was not. I am sure that banana bread was made during those periods, but I don't have any independent recollection. Those bananas would be served until they were all gone. Count on it. Plan for it.

During the months of May and October, you could plan on going to church not only for the morning Mass, but evening devotion in honor of the Blessed Mother. The month of May was especially dedicated to her. During the Pentecost, you could count on more than your share of church sessions. No matter what, one attended church at least once a day. Bare minimum. At certain times of the year, it was not unusual to attend various services three times a day. There was a lot of church attendance during those years.

Another example would be bath night. Bath night was usually Tuesday night for grades 3 and 4, until you got into the upper grades.

Then it went to Saturday night. The younger kids had their bath night on Wednesdays. Movies were always on a Friday night. This establishment was definitely operated in a military fashion. I guess I was getting what the convicts call "stir crazy."

Early in the day, Christmas Eve, I tried to devise a plan. I wanted to celebrate Christmas and my birthday, a few days later, in a different sort of way. I did not know exactly how I would do that, but I did mull over it the entire day. One of the things I considered was running away and "go it alone." I felt that I had enough skills to enable me to survive. Hell, I survived that crap neighborhood in my earlier years. I was able to survive in this godforsaken place. Why can't I survive on the "outside"?

My buddy, Russ Lukes, and I decided that we were low on cigarettes, so we had to go over to Mark's Drugstore. Mark's was located just around the corner from St. Hedwig off Touhy Avenue. It was one of the few places that sold cigarettes to "kids." We snuck out of the orphanage grounds without being seen, traipsed over to the drugstore, and enjoyed a Cherry Coke at the counter. Then I saw it. A huge bourbon display located in the middle of the store just behind the soda fountain. It featured a very sexy woman just beckoning you to taste the brand of bourbon she was pushing. There were over thirty individual quart bottles just waiting to be sampled. Hah! I have never had anything stronger than beer my entire life, and here I was trying to figure out a way to "lift" one of the bottles of bourbon to take back to the orphanage. Per our prearranged plan, Russ diverted Mark's attention while I clumsily slipped a quart of the rotgut bourbon under my bulky coat. At that time, I thought that I was a smooth operator. Little did I know.

As we were walking back to St. Hedwig, Russ asked me if I was successful.

"Of course," I replied and proudly displayed the quart of bourbon for him to see.

It was probably 9:00 p.m., still Christmas Eve, and we were all lounging in the dayroom listening to the radio. The procession would start about 11:00 p.m., with midnight Mass immediately following. We were anxiously waiting, anticipating Christmas Day. Christmas Eve and Christmas Day were big events within the confines of the orphanage. The procession would start things rolling. All inhabitants (or inmates) participated in this annual event. The procession snaked through the building, starting on the first floor, and worked itself to the third floor and then down to the second floor toward the main entrance of the chapel. The procession was led by the band of which I was a part. We may not have been good, but we were able to belt out Christmas music. And the music was recognizable. In fact, most of my classmates were members of the band. I played the euphonium, a rather large baritone horn. Two of my classmates played the clarinet. Another one the saxophone. The tallest guy in our class, Ron Weiss, played the tuba. His horn was bigger than my horn.

We were eagerly looking forward to participating in one of St. Hedwig's most honored traditions preceding the midnight Mass. The first procession I experienced was when I first got to St. Hedwig years ago at the age of eight. It was surreal! The voice of the nuns singing the holy Christmas songs was a real treat, especially when they sang "Silent Night." What a beautiful memory that was. I will never forget it. I do not recall the band playing in that first procession, but they were probably there. This was tradition. After the midnight Mass, the entire student body would partake of a midnight breakfast of scrambled eggs, Polish sausage, and bread and butter. Each person was also served one half of a huge grapefruit. We were given grapefruit once a year, and this was it.

Don't forget that infamous bottle of bourbon. It was sitting just outside the window of the dayroom in the night chill. It's a good thing it was dark. No one was able to see it unless you knew it was there. I carefully selected certain members of my class and asked them to participate in rendering the bottle empty. To the best of my recollection, there were no takers. Russ offered to take a slight sip, but I could tell his heart was not in it. I don't know if they were afraid of being caught or just did not want to screw up Christmas. It did not faze me. I took a few nips of the bourbon—little ones. Then I tried a couple more. At first, it did not seem to have any effect on me. But then it hit me. I experienced what it meant to be "high."

I don't think I had more than four or five sips when I seemed to be floating on air. God, what a feeling that was. It was almost as if I was in another world. But when I checked, I discovered that I was in our dayroom, slightly snockered. The effects were getting more intense. By god, I was going to enjoy this feeling even if my classmates did not want to participate. Then the ominous figure of Father Ed entered the room.

Oh god. I'm caught. Drunk as a skunk. The liquor was really taking its toll. I began muttering to myself. I have got to be real careful about this. What is Father Ed doing in our dayroom on Christmas Eve? Isn't he violating some kind of right? I forgot. We don't have rights in this place. About now the bourbon is really kicking in, making me feel very light-headed and happy. I am ready to walk up to Father Ed and tell him what I think of his overbearing attitude. But no, I don't do it. I remain docile. I am not stupid. Play it out and all will be well. I cannot let the effects of this bourbon affect my judgment.

Father Ed then gets everyone to line up to get their Christmas gift from him and Monsignor Rusch. I somehow got to the rear of the line and tried to behave myself. Have you ever tried to behave while being terribly under the influence of some hard-hitting booze? It was hard, let me tell you. I laughed when I shouldn't have, but no one seemed to notice. I think I was able to pull it off.

Father Ed was passing out five-dollar bills to every member of my class. This was great. Who would have thought that the "Great Disciplinarian" had a heart? This guy was specifically sent to St. Hedwig to induce some discipline, especially on the "boys' side." Apparently, he and the monsignor collaborated and decided to give each of us ninth- and tenth-graders a five-dollar bill for Christmas. Of course, I graciously accepted. I was a bit nervous when Father Ed shook my hand and wished me a Merry Christmas. I don't even remember him handing me the five-dollar bill. I don't think Father Ed suspected anything, at least he did not let on at that time.

The Christmas procession and midnight Mass went off without a hitch. Even some of my friends indicated that I played the baritone like a professional, without a flaw. I myself thought that I have never played my instrument any better. The bandleader, Joe Skubish, did give me a few questioning looks during the procession. I did not think they were admiring looks, but hey, it's Christmas. Enjoy!

After the traditional Christmas morning breakfast of Polish sausage, scrambled eggs, rolls, and grapefruit, I was able to make it to the dormitory about 2:30 a.m. for some much-needed sleep. After all, this was the first time in my life that I really tied one on. I still remember the room turning around when sleep finally overtook my body. What a sound sleep it was.

THE REPRIMAND

It was the first week of January 1955, and Russ Lukes found me in the dining room doing extra chores for Sister Canisia. I guess I was in trouble again and had to perform some extra work for the good sister. I knew she liked me, and I don't know why I always gave her such a hard time. She was probably the mother that I so sorely missed. I liked being around her, but it was always in a penitential setting. Maybe I was a candidate for Joliet State Penitentiary.

"Father Ed wants to see us. Right now," Russ stated. He then went to inform Sister Canisia that we had to go.

"What does Ed want?" I asked.

"I don't know. He just said to get you and meet him in the auditorium below the chapel."

I was concerned just out of habit. Normally, I was able to cover my tracks and not get caught for most infractions. Sister Canisia used to punish me if she even thought I might have done something wrong, whether or not a wrong was actually committed. I must admit that it kept me on my toes. But Father Ed?

One did not mess with Father Ed. He was a mean-looking sort. Probably five foot ten, 190 or so pounds, with a round face and light-colored hair. He could probably hold his own in a street fight. He was downright husky. He could not have been much over thirty-eight years old at that time. I respected the man. I served many a mass for him as an altar boy, but I had not had much to do with him outside the sacristy. I did get an occasional request from Father Ed to play my harmonica. As I recall, his favorite song was "Harbor Lights."

When Russ and I walked into the empty auditorium, Father Ed was standing off to the side, talking to one of the tallest policemen I had ever seen in my life. What I remember most about that cop was the high-top boots that he wore. Most impressive! God, he must have stood well over six foot six. The gun in his holster looked like a cannon. That uniform really looked good on him. Not a wrinkle. But his necktie had a tiny gravy spot. It's funny some of the details that you remember after all these years. That gravy spot just stuck out even though the rest of the regalia was neat and spotless.

Father Ed started giving a sermon about the evils of drinking. He looked at Russ and talked about "guilt by association" and some other stuff that I do not recall. Right then, I knew that I was "busted." Then Father Ed introduced the policeman to us. I extended my hand to shake hands with the gentleman, just like I had been taught, but the policeman just glared at me. He was not friendly. It was time for me to get concerned. Father Ed then left the auditorium with Russ. They left me alone with the cop. I was getting more concerned by the minute.

I was about fifteen years old but felt like a five-year-old. Scared to death but not wanting to show it. The policeman asked me some rather mundane questions about what grade I was in, how I'm doing in school, and if I had ever been in trouble with the "law." Then he hit me with the question.

"Did you take a bottle of bourbon from Mark's Drugstore without paying for it?"

I replied, "What bourbon?" Wrong answer.

I felt a sharp pain on the left side of my head. I never saw it coming, a quick slap for effect. He definitely got my attention. I immediately started babbling about how sorry I was to take the bourbon and that I would pay for it somehow. He turned me into a blithering idiot. I felt that familiar fear of wetting one's pants, but I guess my bladder was in better control than I was. I agreed to go to Mark's Drugstore and apologize to the owner.

I was never so embarrassed in my life. Mark made me feel like a heel. After all, he was always good to us. I had to do some chores at the drugstore for Mark in order to pay off the bourbon. I was able to do this in three sessions after school. Father Ed had me report to him at least once a week just to talk. Then he would hand me several packs of cigarettes that he had confiscated from some of the students at St. Hedwig. He would tell me, "Get rid of these." Father Ed actually treated me pretty well despite what I had done. Sometimes I sold the cigarettes back to their original owners. Usually I kept them for myself and Russ.

A VISIT FROM NANA

In October 1955, an event took place that probably changed the course of my life. It was just after lunch, around one o'clock in the afternoon, when I was summoned to the office. Being summoned to the office was a big event for most of us. It usually meant that there was a death or serious illness in one's family outside the walls of the orphanage. As I walked to the office, I was hoping for good news. Things had not been going that well in the past weeks. I had been incarcerated in this place for about seven and a half years, and I wanted out. I was hoping for some good news, maybe a specific date when I would be leaving this godforsaken place.

As I walked into the office, I noted that Sister Sienna was having a discussion with an older man and a woman. The woman seemed familiar to me. I just could not place her. She wore a black dress and black shoes. The string of pearls around her neck was very attractive. She was very classy looking. Was she some kind of a lost relative? Then it hit me; it was my nana. It was my mom's mother, my grandma. God, I hadn't seen her in probably close to ten years.

"Nana?" I muttered.

"Michael, is that you? My god, it is you. How you've grown."

I ran toward her and gave her a great, big bear hug. When she hugged back, I thought she was going to break my back. She was strong. Nana was a tall, husky woman. She did not want to let go of me. Did that ever feel good. I could not remember the last time I had been hugged. It was probably when I was six or seven years old. I came close to breaking down and crying right then, but too many years and tears had gone by, and I wasn't about to let this reunion break me. I let the "tough guy" in me take over, but it did not fool Nana. She could tell by how hard I was squeezing her back. Nevertheless, the tears never came.

She introduced me to her husband, Alex. I think this was husband number 3. We shook hands like gentlemen despite the fact that I was only fourteen years old. I was not about to let him get too close to me because he was a stranger. He was probably a nice guy, but I had to be careful.

Suddenly, it became very quiet in that office. "Nicklehead," our pet name for Sister Sienna, had disappeared sometime during the reunion and had rounded up my brother and sister, Ray and Sandra. There they were. I made the introductions to Nana, as if she really needed it. Ray was cordial enough, but Sandra was very suspicious. I explained to her who these people were, and she suddenly became afraid. She thought I should have called our dad and let him know that "these people" were here, as if "these people" were enemies. I guess the years of brainwashing had taken their toll. Ray could care less. He was enjoying the moment. He was so used to the attention the nuns paid him that he just ate up Nana's affection. Sandra remained very cool toward Nana and Alex. At least initially. I was hoping she would warm up to them.

Sister Sienna must have picked up on the tension and suggested that we give them a tour of St. Hedwig and show them how we live. I thanked the Lord under my breath for Sister Sienna's suggestion and led my nana and newly found grandpa out of the office and down the corridor. I had to actually beckon Sandra and Ray to follow us. This was so far out of the norm for the three of us. Getting visitors in the middle of the week was an incredible event. It never happened. Wow! I was just loving it. Ray was enjoying it. Sandra remained suspicious.

Being the tour director, I made the most of it. I took Nana and Grandpa Alex on a complete inspection of the entire school. Areas that were normally "off-limits" to the inmates were suddenly open to us. I took them through the girls' and boys' dining halls, the main kitchen, bakery, workers' quarters, laundry room, and even the boiler room. They seemed to enjoy the tour and asked many questions. I noted that class was out and the kids were out on the playgrounds. That was an excuse for me to take my captive audience into the main building of the orphanage and show them the classrooms and the dormitories where we slept. Nana remarked how clean everything seemed to be. I informed her who really kept it clean. Every kid in the place could take some credit for the overall cleanliness.

It was getting close to four o'clock in the afternoon, and Nana indicated that it was time for them to leave. They had a long drive to the south side of Chicago and then on to their home in California. Nana pulled me close to her and whispered to me, "Write a letter to your mother. She is so worried about you."

I assured Nana that I would but that she would have to give me her address. I was also surprised to learn that my mother was living in California. I had heard rumors from various relatives but nothing concrete. This was solid information, and I intended to act on it as soon as I could. I did miss my mom. It had been more years than I could remember. I told Nana that the front office, namely the nuns she had dealt with, would probably confiscate any letters written to me and give them to my dad. Nana said that she would take care of that problem. Nana gave me a business card with my mom's address on the back. I think the business card was that of her attorney whom she had threatened to call earlier.

Nana explained to me that the front-office nuns were not about to let her visit with us when she arrived earlier this day. The nuns told her that my father would not allow visitors from "outside" the family. Apparently, Nana read them the Riot Act and threatened them with a lawsuit. She extremely objected to the term "outside" the family. I think my nana was able to convince Sister Sienna and Sister Aloysius that she was my grandma and that she was entitled to visit us anytime she wanted.

Nana gave me another business card with her address on the back. She asked me to write her a letter once in a while and let her know how they were treating me. I assured her I would write to her and my mom.

Nana suddenly pulled me close to her and gave me another tremendous bear hug. She slipped a rolled-up bill into my hand and admonished me to share it with Ray and Sandra.

Nana then grabbed Ray and gave him a good hug. He hugged back too. It was a good experience for him. Although he did not remember who Nana was, he did acknowledge that she must have been a part of his past. Sandra stood there, hesitantly, not knowing what to do. Nana, in her infinite wisdom, calmly spoke to her and told Sandra she would not tell anyone if Sandra wanted a hug. Sandra slowly walked up to Nana and very carefully opened her arms. Nana smothered her with a bear hug, and it finally took hold. Sandra succumbed to the hug and started crying. She must have been feeling good about the hug because those had to be tears of joy. She was crying harder and harder. After a few minutes, she was able to compose herself, and she dried off the tears with Nana's handkerchief. I think Nana just made a friend. I felt good about that because Sandra had been so standoffish most of the visit. Nana knew how to handle her and had her smiling in no time.

But they had to leave us. I saw Nana shed a tear or two. Alex offered to drive, but she was having none of that. Finally, she got into her car (1955 Chevrolet with cream top and green body), started it up, waved one last time, and drove toward the exit on Touhy Avenue.

I could not handle the suspense anymore as I watched them make their turn into the traffic toward Harlem Avenue. I had to see the denomination of that bill without Ray and Sandra seeing it. I don't think they saw Nana give the bill to me, but I did not feel like sharing at that moment. I slowly unfurled the greenback and discovered it was a fifty-dollar bill. I don't remember ever seeing a fifty-dollar bill in my life. Wow! I felt like I was rich. The most my dad had ever given me was $5. And I think that was for graduation from eighth grade.

What a day! What a visit! I had such a good feeling about everything. And the money gave me a power I had never experienced. I finally relented and gave $10 each to Ray and Sandra. It took me three days to make that decision. I felt that they were entitled to some of it.

Ray had no idea who those people were. Sandra may have had an idea, but she hadn't been all that friendly. I knew the significance of that visit and knew that things in my personal life would never be the same. Prior to this visit, I did not have any idea how to contact my mother. Now I knew.

It was about a month later when I was summoned to the front office. When I walked in, Sister Sienna warmly greeted me and informed me that I had a letter from California. She handed it to me with the seal still intact. The envelope was thick. I still remember that peculiar greenish color of ink that adorned the envelope with my name and the address of St. Hedwig. I reached out to accept the envelope, and Sister Sienna actually winked at me. I always thought she hated me. How nice. I wonder if my nana had anything to do with that. I accepted the envelope as calmly as I could and did an about-face a little quicker than I really wanted to. I wanted to get out of that office and go find a nice, quiet corner so I could read the letter. The return address was my nana's. I got outside the door of the main building and ran toward the playground area. Just beyond the playing children were several benches. They were a little out of the way of the playground, thus affording me some privacy. I sat down at the nearest bench and tore open the envelope. I removed about seven pages of the letter. I hadn't even read the letter, and I was ecstatic. My nana wrote several pages, mostly talking about her trip back to California after she and Alex had visited us. She really enjoyed our visit, and she was looking forward to the time I would go and visit her in California. A couple of months ago, that thought would never have crossed my mind, but now it seemed that it was a definite possibility. I couldn't stay in St. Hedwig much beyond my eighteenth birthday, not if I had anything to do with it.

I continued on with the letter. Nana signed off, and then I noted that there was a different handwriting on the remaining three pages. I read on and found out that my mother had written me a letter. I could not tell you all that it said, but it did make me feel like I had not been forgotten. She indicated a desire to see me and hoped that we could see each other soon. I knew that it would not be in the foreseeable future, but at least it was something to hang on to. It was definitely something to look forward to. It was a very nice letter. She mostly told me how much she liked living in California. I think she told me about her job and her husband, Lee. She had been married to him for about eight years, and she wanted me to meet him someday. I must have read that letter about five or six times before supper. And then I read it again, once or twice, afterward.

I never heard from my mom after that first letter. I did not dare answer it. If my dad found out, I would be dead meat. He would probably kill me. My dad had been telling my brother and sister that our mother was dead. He actually had them convinced that she was killed in a car accident years ago. Of course, I knew better. And then the visit from Nana really sparked my interest, which in turn sparked their interest. In time, I was able to convince Ray and Sandra that their mother, our mother, was alive and well and living in California. They eventually told my dad, and I had to deal with the consequences. Things were never the same between my dad and me. That really upset him, the fact that I told Ray and Sandra the truth about our mother. Nana, on the other hand, continued to send me an occasional letter. She always gave me an update on my mom and Lee, and they did understand why I could not write to them just yet. I did write to Nana and tried to let her know what was going on in our lives. She was always afraid that we would fall out of touch. I promised and promised her in my letters that I would always remember their address. If she ever moved, she was going to have to let me know somehow.

About three months after Nana's visit, one of the nuns in the front office had accidentally, or on purpose, given my dad one of Nana's letters to me. It was unopened when it was given to my dad. Of course, he read the letter, ripped it up, and admonished me to never write to "that woman" again. Well, I had to let Nana know. I wrote her one last time and promised that they would hear from me as soon as I was able to do it without getting into trouble. I personally thought my dad was being unreasonable.

About a year later, in the fall of 1956, the three of us were removed from the "prison" called St. Hedwig. Apparently, the administration had gotten wind that my father had remarried, and the Catholic Church did not recognize this union. Furthermore, his children—Michael, Sandra, and Raymond—were no longer welcome at St. Hedwig.

Regardless of the circumstances, we were so glad to get out of that place and start a new life. One of the first items of business I took care of was to write to my nana and inform her of our new address and for her to please be patient. I had a feeling I would be seeing them within the next couple of years. My nana could not let me know that she got the letter, but I knew in my heart that she knew and that she was looking forward to our next visit.

ORPHANS VERSUS ST. CHARLES

From my very first day at St. Hedwig Orphanage, the almost-new gymnasium fascinated me. There was a single regulation basketball court with a permanent basket at one end. At the opposite end was a mobile basket, attached to the upper beams of the gymnasium roof with cables holding it in place. This basket could be raised or lowered, depending on the usage of the gym. On occasion, the gym was used as an auditorium. Other times, it was used for regular basketball games with plenty of room for spectators. This gymnasium was also the location for our Friday-night movies. The building was large enough to comfortably seat the entire population of St. Hedwig School, which was approximately six hundred students plus the staff. At Christmastime, the various charity organizations used the gym to dole out Christmas presents. To get maximum usage, there were two short basketball courts, which intersected the main court. This allowed two basketball games to be played at the same time. During inclement weather, basketball games were a constant activity.

In years past, long before my tenure at St. Hedwig, the school had a very colorful history of basketball championships in the Chicago area. This was evident by the numerous trophies and pictures displayed in the main building of St. Hedwig. Some of the tournaments were sponsored by the CYO (Catholic Youth Organization). I specifically remember a man by the name of Jules Pandera who helped coach our team. He was a good friend of Fr. Bill Wozniak. Together, they tried to resurrect a waning basketball program.

Jules had been one of the orphanage's stars in days gone by. He now was a part-time coach for us kids. He turned us on to the game of basketball while we were very young, probably twelve years old. At this particular time in our lives, we were in the freshman or sophomore year of high school, probably fifteen and sixteen years old. Our center was a towering six-foot-one-inch classmate by the name of Ron Weiss. Other team members included Eddie, Russ, and Frankie "the Flash." Frankie was only five foot two, but he could steal a ball from an opponent at will. He was also a good point guard. I don't recall the other members of my team. They could have included Steve, Richard, Ronald, Ron, and maybe even the brothers Frank and Freddie.

Jules and Father Bill drilled us incessantly. It seemed that all of our free time was consumed by basketball. Believe me, we were not complaining. We were part of the older boys' group and, as such, looked up to by the younger boys. We were heroes to those youngsters. Our team participated in several tournaments, and we all got to play. I do not recall whether we won or lost. I just remember that our team played well. Ronnie, our center, was our best player. He was also our best free thrower. I faintly remember Jules and Father Bill introducing us to zone defense. I was a slow learner, so I had to sit on the bench a lot. Besides, I was convinced that Father Bill did not like me.

One day at practice, Jules told us that we were going to play a basketball game at St. Charles, Illinois. To me, St. Charles was just a name of a city. I had no idea what we were getting into. Slowly, the word trickled down to us that St. Charles was a reform school for boys. Bad boys. Boys who had committed robberies and burglaries. Maybe even murder. The facility was called the Illinois Youth Center. Our coaches were not telling us much. Even on the drive up there, Father Bill and Jules did not enlighten us further.

We talked among ourselves that this was just another basketball game and that we were going to win. Our positive thoughts were suddenly cast aside when we approached the gated facility. As our station wagon drove onto the premises, we could see guard towers silhouetted against the fading sunlight. It was probably 7:00 p.m., just after supper. I could make out the forms of guards in their respective towers. I felt like our team was going to be dessert for these criminals. Then I saw the first guard at the vehicle entrance. Whether he had a shotgun or a rifle, I do not recall. It was the biggest, meanest, scariest gun I ever saw in my life. He wasn't even holding it. It was in some sort of gun rack.

We were ushered past their security checkpoint without our duffel bags being checked. I think the guards saw how scared we were. They treated us well. Then there was another security checkpoint. That also went smoothly. We were shown a large locker room with showers. The lockers appeared to be new and unused compared to the decrepit lockers we had back on our campus. There were a lot of loud voices on the other side of a partition separating us from the criminals. The voices were probably our opponents getting ready for the slaughter of the innocents.

After we had donned our ragtag uniforms, we were ready to take warm-ups on the basketball court. As we entered the gymnasium with great trepidation, we saw large groups of boys and young men being ushered to their seats. There were large bleacher-type benches on two sides of the gym similar to the ones we had in our gym. However, these bleachers were designed to hold a lot of people. There were probably twenty rows of seats going up and running the entire length of the basketball court. It looked like we were going to be playing basketball in front of a lot of people, probably the biggest crowd in our young lives.

Our team was busily trying to get rid of the jitters by doing organized layups when the St. Charles team entered the gymnasium. The audience boisterously welcomed their team with shouting and clapping. When we looked over at our opponents, we got the shock of our young lives. Every player appeared to be well over six feet tall with some closer to seven feet. All but two of their basketball players were black. A strange feeling of intimidation swept over us. Not only were we nervous, we were also scared. All the horror stories we had heard about black people were now becoming reality in our very sheltered lives. Most of us had never been that close to a black person before now.

Suddenly our team started missing the practice layups. No one should ever miss a layup, especially in practice. And to top it off, their team was wearing the nicest, brightest, most colorful uniforms.

Their basketball shorts matched their tops. This IYC team looked like a million dollars compared to ours.

Father Bill called us over to the sidelines. He seemed unaffected by it all. He talked to us like he usually talked to us in our practices. His even-tempered voice would normally calm us down in a crisis, but not this time. All team members exchanged nervous looks. Ron, our center, appeared to have lost all the color in his face. Russ did not look any better. I was frozen. I did not move. Thank God, I was not a starter. We all wished we were somewhere else.

We sat on the sidelines and watched St. Charles warm up. They did not appear to be as organized as our team. Missed layups were the norm. Our team appeared ready to breathe a collective sigh of relief. That's when we saw them, two players who seemed to have exceptional ability. They never missed a practice layup shot. It seemed that they did not miss any type of shot they took. We still had the jitters.

The referees came onto the court to a chorus of boos and hisses. The head ref blew his whistle to signal the teams to take their positions on the court. Our center, Ron, actually had to look up at their center. He must have hit six feet six inches, minimum. The other starters appeared to be over six feet. All players took their positions. The ref insisted that all players shake hands. None of the inmates seemed friendly. They must have had their game faces on. God help us. We were going to need all the help we could get.

Suddenly the game was underway. St. Charles got the tip, and their player dribbled straight to the basket and scored. St. Hedwig now had the ball and took it down court. After several passes, the ball was fed to Ron for a quick two points. We did not know it at the time, but St. Hedwig would not fall behind again for the rest of the game. Five minutes into the game, despite the size difference in teams, it became apparent that we were the superior team. St. Hedwig players did one fast break after another. Rebounding was also going our way. St. Hedwig began to dominate the boards. By halftime, the orphans were ahead of the inmates by eighteen points.

When the second half started, the orphans still dominated. Frankie stole the ball from a St. Charles player three times in a row. Each time, the ball was flipped to Ron for a score. St. Charles began to play more aggressively, but to no avail. They began fouling our players consistently. Most of the St. Hedwig players were proficient in free throws. This helped add to the lead. At one point, the spectators began cheering for our team every time we scored. This game was becoming a route despite our earlier fears. The more we scored, the more our confidence grew. By the time the last basket was made, this most unlikely team made many friends in the reformatory. The crowd lustily cheered for the orphans long after the last points were scored.

We were glad the game was over. We just hoped the opposing team did not find their way into our locker room. They seemed friendly enough after the game, but we all took a quick shower and got dressed in record time. We actually thought some of the other team would cause us trouble before we got out of the confines of that prison. Our group was never so glad to see the large metal doors open for our departure. When we hit the main highway for the return to St. Hedwig's, it seemed that Father Bill drove a little faster than he normally would. After a few miles, we all began to lighten up and enjoy the moment and the rest of the ride "home."

THE HUNGARIAN CONNECTION

In October 1956, shortly before I left St. Hedwig, a significant event took place that would affect the lives of many people at St. Hedwig Orphanage. If I may, I would like to throw in a little history at this point.

Earlier in the year, Nikita Khrushchev, premier of the Soviet Union, began the de-Stalinization process wherein he discredited the former premier, Josef Stalin, and made public the many errors committed by the Stalin regime. The Soviets chose to call the process the New Course. The people of Hungary mistook the actions to mean that they had political freedom in sight, but such was not the case. Public demonstrations and political infighting were taking place in Hungary for months when it finally came to a head in October 1956. Masses of people rose violently against the communist regime and took to the streets to demand their freedom. Week after week, the demonstrations became bigger and more forceful. The communist government collapsed, and a new Hungarian premier was named to lead the newly formed government at the end of October.

However, a week later, on November 4, some 2,500 Soviet tanks entered the capital of Hungary. Thousands died in street fighting, and 150,000 fled across the border into Austria. The Soviets had taken back what was mistakenly interpreted as a newly formed government of

Hungary. The communist leaders forcefully reestablished their hold on a country long suffering under Soviet influence.

As a result, a group of refugees from Hungary were brought to the United States. After all the smoke had cleared, there were several teenage refugees, orphans, who had no place to call home. They had no known relatives in this country. About seven of them had found themselves at St. Hedwig Orphanage. Rumor had it that these seven were unruly and hard-nosed and could not be controlled by any authority. The so-called disciplinarians at St. Hedwig were custom-made for the new refugees.

I had overheard several nuns discussing the refugees. Several of them had been known to have killed Russian soldiers using Molotov cocktails, hence their political asylum status. All of them were true orphans and had lived on the street for months and months before coming to the United States. Two of these refugees were assigned to the eighth grade. The others were placed in appropriate classes depending on their age and education. All spoke broken English.

One of these kids, Janus (or Janek), was assigned to my dinner table along with my brother Ray and my sister Sandra. It was somewhat of an experience. My father was of Polish heritage, but my mother was full-blooded, red-hot Hungarian. I made this fact known to Janus, and we immediately hit it off. His lack of command of the English language did not slow us down. He even had a sense of humor after one got to know him.

In discussing his situation, I found out that he had been orphaned about a year earlier and had lived on the streets in the shadow of Russian imperialism. Both of his parents had been shot by a Russian firing squad for "crimes against the people." This fourteen-year-old had deep-set eyes, which made him appear much older than he was. He was tall and stocky and walked with a purpose. He never seemed to smile. I imagined that he had seen a lot of suffering and sadness before coming to St. Hedwig. I really focused on Janus because he seemed to have more problems than I did at the time. I believe he had a sibling, but I am not sure if it was a male or a female. Janus kept to himself and never had too much to say to others. He spent his free time with the other refugees whenever possible.

One morning at breakfast, I noted that he kept eyeing the other nearby tables. He ignored me when I asked him what he was looking for. I had learned to respect his silence. There was usually a good reason for his actions. After breakfast, I watched him from a distance go from table to table and retrieve the leftover pieces of bread. This was understandable to me because he was used to fending for himself. He never knew when and where his next meal would be.

What happened next though really got my attention. The main ingredient for this breakfast was peanut butter. It was served to each table in a large bowl. Janus took his hand and scooped out all the leftover peanut butter. He then carefully placed the peanut butter in his front pants pocket. He repeated this at two other tables. Afterward, he licked his fingers clean.

Apparently, this foraging had been going on for some time. Not only with Janus, but with the other refugees, both boys and girls. They were hoarding the bread and whatever else they could get their hands on and creating a rodent problem. For the first time in memory, numerous mice were observed on the top floor of St. Hedwig Orphanage. It did not take long for the sisters to figure out who and what the problem was. Once the refugees realized that there would always be three meals a day, no matter what, they relaxed their daily routine of foraging and enjoyed the perks of their newly adopted home. It appeared that they also made friendships with others much easier. They did not have to worry about food anymore. They did not have to concern themselves with where they would shelter for the night. It took a while but they finally settled in at their new home, St. Hedwig Orphanage.

Several weeks later, I left St. Hedwig to go live with my father and his new wife. I have often wondered what became of those orphaned Hungarian Freedom Fighters.

WELCOME HOME

It was October 1956, our first weekend at home after spending eight years in St. Hedwig Orphanage. Both my brother and sister had been incarcerated with me at the orphanage, and we were hell-bent on making a good impression on our new stepmother. We wanted to let her and our dad sleep on this Saturday morning. We wanted to give them a bit of a break. The three of us got ready for the day's chores. Without being asked, Sandra, who was twelve years old, gathered up all the dirty clothing and linen. It was sorted and piled for the washing machine. The washing machine itself was one of those reel types where you had to hand-feed clothes into the ringer in order to squeeze out the excess water. I don't think the spin-dry cycle had been born yet. Sandra had much experience in handling this type of machine, thanks to the constant training by the nuns at St. Hedwig. She was busy doing the clothes, washing and rinsing and running them through the reel-type wringer. It was a tedious job for her age, but she could handle it well.

My ten-year-old brother, Raymond, elected to tackle the kitchen. The dishes from last night's supper were piled on the sink. Dirty pots and pans were set on the stove. He had his work cut out for him, but he too was well trained by the nuns. He knew how to clean a pot or a pan. And dishes? He was an expert. His orphanage training was paying off.

I tackled the rest of the house. The living room and den were a total mess. Newspapers and magazines were strewn all over the place. I made good use of the carpet sweeper so as not to awaken my dad and stepmother. After about forty-five minutes of uninterrupted labor, the den and living room were looking good. Even the throw pillows were fluffed and repositioned on the sofa.

I went into the kitchen to check on my brother and discovered that he had matters well in hand. He did mutter something about making it a family rule not to let dirty dishes set out overnight. After much scrubbing, he had the place spotless. He was in the process of putting the cleaned dishes and silverware away in their appropriate places.

I glanced into the utility room and noted that my sister was busy feeding soggy washed clothes through the wringer. A stick had to be used to help push the clothes through the wringer because the water was very, very hot. The clothes dryer was going full bore with its first load. Everybody had their job to do and did it without complaint.

It was approaching noontime when our stepmother charged into the kitchen and let out a shriek that was hurtful to the ears.

"What the hell is going on here? What are you kids doing?" she hollered. "Nobody told you kids to do anything. You're taking my job away from me. Who the hell do you think you are?"

Being the oldest and self-appointed spokesman, I said, "We're just doing our chores. We're glad to be here and are trying to show our appreciation."

I tried to reason with her and stated, "Look, we are just so glad to be out of that place. This is the first real home we have ever experienced in a long time. We are trying to show our thanks to you and Dad. We know you two work all week. We go to school. The least we can do is try to keep the place clean and orderly. Sandra knows laundry. She knows how to handle the machines, and she knows how to fold the clothes."

"What?" she yelled.

She walked rapidly toward the utility room where Sandra was busy taking a load out of the dryer. *Whapp!* I could not believe what I heard, but I think she just hit my sister. I ran toward the utility room just in time to see my stepmother getting ready to take another punch at the cowering Sandra. The young girl appeared stunned from the blow.

"Stop!" I yelled.

She turned toward me and charged like a rhino, arms flailing. This may have been a woman, but she had some real fists on the end of those arms. I was not about to be struck by them. I deflected the first onslaught effectively. I do believe she hurt herself, but the anger was so intense that she tried to hit me again. Once again, I was able to deflect her swinging fist. Would you believe that she was going to try it a third time? That was when my dad walked into the kitchen and demanded to know what was going on.

"These goddamn kids are taking over the house. You better do something about it. I am not going to stand for it. No goddamn kids are going to run my life," my stepmother uttered.

My dad very feebly tried to reason with her. He kept saying things like, "We've got to learn to get along with one another if we're going to live here." I could tell it was a losing battle for him. He lost control at that time. In fact, I don't think he ever had control. It was plain to see that we three kids were in for a long haul, and it was not going to be pleasant.

My stepmother stood at about five foot eight inches and 180 pounds. I was also five foot eight inches but only 140 pounds. I was just a fifteen-year-old kid. She was a twenty-two-year-old woman who had just been discharged from the United States Air Force. Give me a break. I personally did not want to go one-on-one with her. I would get creamed.

The rest of that day was spent in a fog. Not much else was done by us. My stepmother finished the laundry, cursing and yelling the entire time. The three of us kids spent some time together, not saying much of anything. After a while, Sandra went into her own room and sobbed for the longest time. My father seemed to disappear. I found him later looking under the hood of his car. He seemed to be doing a lot of thinking. I do not recall that he was actually doing anything to the vehicle. I attempted conversation with him, but he was not responsive. It was at that moment I reached the conclusion that he was in a situation that was out of his control. This caused me to lose a lot of respect for him.

We had been released from the orphanage earlier in the week. The administration had discovered that my father had remarried, and in the eyes of the Catholic administrators of St. Hedwig Orphanage, my father was living in sin. They informed him that his offspring, my siblings and I, were no longer welcome at the orphanage. This may have supported his argument that this was in fact a boarding school and not an orphanage. They insisted he remove his children from the premises as soon as possible.

I suppose my father could have walked away from the situation. He could have dropped out of sight, never to be heard from again. The hell with the kids. Leave them in the orphanage. The state of Illinois would take care of the kids. The state would not let the orphanage turn the kids into the street with no place to go, would they? I would not have blamed my father if he had disappeared, but that was not him. He would try to do what was right, whatever that might be. He and my stepmother had just bought a house. Yes, a real house. Not a trailer or a mobile home, but a real house. It was brand-new in a real neighborhood with other families around. It became apparent that my brother, sister, and I were not in the original plans when they moved into the new house. At any rate, the orphanage dropouts were real residents of the Country Club Hills home.

My, what a fancy name for our neighborhood, Country Club Hills. There wasn't a hill in sight. Not even a little one. There was no country club either. I suppose that the developer was hard up for a name. All three of us kids were determined to make things work, no matter what. We were in this together, and if we worked together, we would get through it in grand fashion. I truly believed we could do this in spite of our stepmother.

Over the next couple of years, the five of us generally got along to a point. I truly believed the adults did attempt, in their own way, to ease the situation. It took some doing to deal with the frequent yelling of our stepmother. My siblings and I still remained some sort of a threat to the domain of stepmotherhood. Every once in a while, the tension would get to all of us individually, but rarely simultaneously. Yes, there were minor sporadic clashes over trivial matters. These incidents usually blew over quickly. The three of us did walk on eggshells for the duration.

Entering the junior year of high school, I accepted the fact that I was stuck in that house until I graduated. Being the oldest, I was able to spend a lot of time away from that house. I worked part-time at the nursery tending to plants and assisting the owner with other chores for $1 an hour. After school, I drove up to Clines Nursery at

183rd Street and Cicero Avenue. When my work was over, I did not go straight home. I usually stopped at a friend's house just around the corner from my own. Her mom and dad practically adopted me. I did not exactly abandon my brother and sister in those times, but I did not do much to enhance the relationship either. I erroneously thought that the two of them were very busy with schoolwork. Our stepmother seemed to back off on most control issues and left the two of them alone. She would never forgive me for standing up to her.

When I graduated from Bremen High School in June of 1958, I looked upon the occasion as a milestone in my life. Going on to college was never an option, so I looked toward the military as my next step. I joined the United States Army for a three-year stint of service in July of that year. I immediately reestablished contact with my mother and actually had a tearful reunion with her in October of that same year.

Unknown to me, this was when the troubles really started at our humble abode in Country Club Hills. Sandra, who had always been my biggest supporter, began to receive the brunt of the abuse. Her big brother was no longer there to protect her. She certainly could not rely on our father for any realistic protection. She wrote to me at my base in Fort Leonard Wood, Missouri. Every letter indicated that she was slapped and punched with frequency by our father's wife. Ray seemed to come out from all of this unscathed. Neither Sandra nor I could recall any abuse directed toward him. It appeared that Ray was the "chosen one."

When Sandra graduated from high school, she found out that our father and stepmother had no intention of financing her way through college. In fact, they wanted her to help pay expenses in the household. She had dreams of going to medical school. She certainly was intelligent enough to do it. As a result, Sandra found out about a nursing school in Harvey, Illinois, that would help her with her education. Sandra jumped at the chance to take advantage of the offer and trained to become an x-ray technician. This became her realistic ticket out of the abusive situation in which she was living.

In retrospect, I can now look back and immediately see what the main problems were. The orphanage administration found out too soon about the remarriage. This forced us out prematurely, putting pressure on the new marriage of my dad and stepmother. They, especially my stepmother, were not ready for three teens to invade their humble home. There was also the issue of age between my stepmother and me. She was only twenty-two. I was fifteen. Most importantly, all three of us kids were trained by the nuns to be independent. That was the Hedwigian way. We were taught to live life and be a productive member of society. The nuns did a good job. I guess that was a threat to our "beloved" stepmother. She wanted to be in control.

ONE LAST LOOK—1996

Word came to me that the St. Hedwig Orphanage Alumni Association was going to have one last luncheon before the contractors razed the buildings at St. Hedwig Orphanage, 7135 N. Harlem Avenue, Niles, Chicago, Illinois. The Pontarelli brothers of Chicago had purchased the property from the archdiocese of Chicago with the intention of building a massive condo complex in its place. There had been ten or twelve of these luncheons over the years, and I had yet to attend one. This one was going to be special because after the luncheon, all who cared were going to take one last walking tour of "our home," the orphanage grounds. The luncheon was scheduled for October 20, 1996, at the White Eagle Restaurant in Niles, Illinois. The fact that I lived in Florida was not going to prevent me from attending this event.

I contacted the coordinator, Rose Killips, who herself was an alumna of St. Hedwig. Even though I had never met her, talking to her on the telephone was like talking to a very dear friend. I asked her what normally occurred at this type of event, and I was a bit disturbed by her answer. She told me that the ex-students of St. Hedwig would arrive individually, engage in small talk, partake of the buffet lunch, finish eating, and break into small groups. The nuns, who were always invited, arrived together, sat at their own tables, enjoyed the food, and visited among themselves after the meal. After a short time, everyone then left just like they had arrived. This was all done quietly and in low key. There was not much interaction among most of the group. Looking around the room, one could sense that some of the diners wanted to socialize a bit more, but their shyness prevented it. And there was not much interaction with the nuns, most of which were quite elderly at this time. Rose went on to tell me that she wanted to do things differently this time in order to make a real social event materialize.

I asked her if it would be all right if I spoke to the group for a few minutes, sort of take them down memory lane and talk about some familiar incidents and people. Rose reminded me that I was dealing with a tough audience but that I could take all the time I wanted. The way she wished me luck made me think to myself, *Why am I doing this? Am I crazy?*

It was about two months to zero hour, and I had no idea how I was going to pull this off. "Stick to what you know and you can't go wrong," I kept telling myself. Finally, I had a plan and began making my notes for the presentation.

October 20 arrived with a burst of glory. Days prior to the event had featured some dismal weather, but this day was great. The sun shone brighter than usual. My brother-in-law, Dick, was the self-appointed chauffeur, my sister Sandra the navigator for the one-and-a-half-hour trip to Chicago from their home in Kankakee, south of Chicago. My wife Sandi and I occupied the backseat. I looked over my notes several times during the trip but still felt that I was treading into uncharted waters. How would it go? Rose did say that they would be a tough audience. All those years of impromptu speaking engagements with the LAPD should make it easy for me. Wrong! I was as nervous as a young bride. I had hosted and toasted more than a few retirement parties with good success. Why the jitters?

When we entered the dining hall where the event was going to take place, my sister spotted Rose making last-minute adjustments for the luncheon. She was making arrangements to have the nuns escorted to various tables throughout the large room. This was going to be a social event, period. Sandra introduced Rose to Sandi and me, and we liked her immediately. She asked if I was prepared to give my little talk. I hemmed and hawed, and before I could speak, she stated, "You've got to. We are counting on you." There was no question about it. I was going to give a talk whether I wanted to or not.

The array of Polish food was outstanding, according to those who could eat it. I was having difficulty trying to partake because of my nervousness. I ate some, picked at it a lot, tried a little more. Before you knew it, the emcee of the affair, Don Killips, gave me the signal that I was next to appear at the podium. Rose introduced me to the gathering of about 160 orphanage alumni and spouses, friends, guests, priests, and nuns. As I walked up to the podium, I thought my legs were going to fail me. I felt like I was walking in about three feet of water. I just know I would break into a cold sweat and would probably pass out when I touched the microphone. I heard this surreal noise and was wondering what it was. Then it dawned on me that it was applause for the next speaker, me.

I reached into my pocket for the notes I had so carefully typed and discovered that they were GONE. Oh my god! Then I saw my wife Sandi waving my precious notes. I had left them at the table. Rose retrieved the notes and handed them to me. How was I going to get through this?

"My name is Mike Krecioch. I was a resident of St. Hedwig from October 1948 to October 1956. Bear with me as I try to take you down 'memory lane.' I remember taking a bath 'by the numbers.' Probably twenty kids per tub. You hit the big time when you got into the older grades and were allowed to take a private bath. That happened about the fifth or sixth grade."

I could feel a twitter run through the group as I spoke. Several eyes of those that did remember those famous group baths lit up.

"I remember Friday-night movies," I continued, "with Joe Skubish providing organ music while we anxiously awaited the start of the film. I remember the 'duck pond,' a small, outdoor swimming pool, which was only three feet deep at its deepest end. And Gorky Hill in the wintertime. It really wasn't much of a hill."

By now most of the 160 strong were acknowledging in one way or another their remembrance of the various events I spoke about. A certain excitement seemed to surge through the crowd as they leaned closer toward me as if to listen better. This seems to be going really well.

I continued on. "I remember Camp Villa Marie and my first grilled hamburger. What an exciting time in my life! I was probably eight years old at the time. I remember Mr. Paul, the resident carpenter and night watchman. I don't think he liked anybody. Do any of you remember Bob Dillinger (Lukowski) and his roundhouse curve ball? Then there was Sister Odilia, a real fanatic of the Chicago Cubs. Farmer Joe. He was the one who taught me to drive a dump truck. In fact, I almost wrecked it. Sister Felicia was my third- and fourth-grade dormitory nun. She was the first person to ever have the guts to call me 'Mikey' to my face. You all may remember Paczki Day, but do you remember Punczki Day? Remember Jeep? He made it all happen in the bakery. The donuts and the cookies. I will never forget that man. How about Dr. Rosa? Do you recall who he was? Yep, he was the dentist. Many of us would do everything in our power to avoid visiting him. Every Wednesday he was there. Does anyone remember the annual field day? It occurred in the gymnasium and featured tricycle races with the bigger kids. Very entertaining stuff. The evening would be topped off by the finals of the free throw contest."

Looking around the audience, I noted that there appeared to be a lot of interest in what I was talking about. People were smiling and acknowledging what I was saying. This was not what Rose told me would happen, but yet it was happening. A spark of life had come over this group, and it was getting more and more animated. I was really loving this. I then continued on with my journey down memory lane.

"Do you remember midnight procession at Christmastime? The midnight Mass and the fabulous breakfast afterward? Remember? Polish sausage and scrambled eggs? And grapefruit? How about Bill Biel's 1955 Oldsmobile, white over red with power steering, the newest gadget on a car? The exciting tunnels. All of them. The dining room tunnel and the gym tunnel were the most used. And then there was Sister Edith. I really believe that woman invented whitewash just to keep my buddy Russ and me from getting into trouble. Those beautiful white rocks, which adorned the grounds did not get white by themselves. Does anyone remember the mayonnaise parties? Just a loaf of bread and mayonnaise. Mmmmmmm. How about the Hungarian refugees in 1956? There were a few of them who were placed in St. Hedwig. We had a printshop. Remember some of the people who worked there? There was Marion Matuszak, Bruno 'Jake' Wadas. I myself ran the Gordon Press when I was fourteen years old. Sister Leonette ran the little candy store. And Sister Lorriane tried to make a draftsman out of me. Remember Father Ed? How about Father Bill? And Elmer? Everyone remembers Father Rusch. I can still smell his cigar smoke floating in the corridors. How about the Knights of Columbus and the Ladies of Isabella at Christmastime? And speaking of that, remember the American Legion Drum and Bugle Corps? Their music was the best. Does anyone remember the Stopka twins, Frank and Freddie? They were icons to me and my classmates because they were a few years older. We really did look up to them. They even played football at Holy Trinity High School. And there was the skating rink. Remember the road to St. Andrew? That was the official skating rink. And the potato-peeler machine. You had to keep an eye on it or watch the potatoes disappear. Eighth-grade graduation was always a big deal. The year I graduated, 1954, it was powder blue suits, black boxer neckties, boxer shoes, and 'Mr. B' shirts. And the pants had to be pegged. Eighth-grade graduation was probably the biggest event that would occur for most of us while living at St. Hedwig. Do you remember?"

Some of the people in the crowd were dabbing at tears. Apparently, I hit on a few soft spots, and it showed. I perceived that this was an appropriate time to wind down, so I began to do so.

"I want to give thanks to all the sisters who got me through one of the toughest times of my life. They were responsible for keeping me on the straight and narrow path. I especially want to thank Sister Marcy. She is one of the finest educators and humanitarians that I have had the privilege of knowing."

I walked toward my table, and the place erupted in deafening applause. Several people reached out to me to shake my hand or just touch me. I was very moved by their gestures. Suddenly another person ran up to the podium and wanted to tell a little story about her experiences at St. Hedwig. And then another and another. It was rather uplifting to see and experience. I can't recall exactly what they talked about, but it was along the same lines as my talk. They were all positive experiences.

At this time, Rose Killips introduced Sister Angelita, one of the nuns I remembered as being at St. Hedwig. She had composed a fairy tale that she wanted to share with the audience. The title of the fairy tale is "The Children's Village." I had a feeling that this was going to be something special. You could have heard a pin drop as she read the story.

The Children's Village

Once upon a time, there was a children's village. In the village, there were many buildings: some large, some small. They were built on a large tract of land adjoining a cemetery. The village provided accommodations needed to live a life of security. There was a large chapel, a dining hall, living quarters, elementary school, and a two-year high school, a combination gymnasium and auditorium, a kitchen, bakery, laundry, small hospital, swimming pool, library, rumpus room, many parlors, and plenty of land to enjoy the fresh air of an open field.

By now, you must be eager to know who lived in this special village. Well, since the tale is about a children's village, everything in the village was for the children. Very small children, bigger children, and very big children. They came there for many different reasons and made the village their home.

Wherever you find children, there must be someone to guide them, teach them, protect them, and provide for their needs; so in the village, there were sisters who took care of them. Whenever we speak about sisters, they are people who serve the Lord and help him in guiding others to love God and obey his laws. There was a headmaster, whose responsibility was to see that everything operated properly and efficiently.

I mentioned a chapel. Here, the children came to celebrate Mass and to pray and observe the liturgical seasons of the year. They sang beautifully and enjoyed singing to such an extent that the windows vibrated when they sang. The children had the opportunity to participate in processions in the chapel and on the grounds of the village on Corpus Christi Day. On these occasions, the sisters dressed the little girls in beautiful white dresses and the little boys in page-boy suits. The boys' caps were adorned with colorful plumes. They looked like the pages who served the kings of their countries from days gone by. These little children served the King of Heaven and Earth.

The school was located right in the main building. There was no need for the children to travel by bus. They studied all the prescribed subjects assigned for each grade. In class, the sisters prepared them for their first confession, their first Holy Communion, Confirmation, and the basic fundamentals of the Catholic Church.

For meals, the children assembled in a large dining room. Three hot meals a day were provided. At ten in the morning and right after school, the sisters were happy to provide snacks of cookies, biscuits, and fruit. Memorable in the history of the village was PACZKI DAY, a few days before Christmas. Children received a shopping bag of clothing and goodies. The village was filled with laughter and excitement while the gifts were unwrapped. On the feast day of St. Hedwig, the bakery provided the children with special cream puffs. In the early years of the village, a section of land was designated for farming. The children had fun picking tomatoes, carrots, cucumbers, and turnips. They enjoyed the crunch of a crisp carrot. When ill, the children were taken to the infirmary building where nurses cared for them.

The combination gymnasium and auditorium gave the older boys an opportunity to become skilled in athletics. They competed with other teams for the enjoyment of the entire village. The auditorium enabled the children to get a taste of the fine arts as they entertained visitors by participating in stage plays and dances.

A swimming pool refreshed them during the summer months. A library made it possible for them to do research work and provide an abundance of reading materials. The recreation room was a place for noisy and exciting games. On Friday, the auditorium became a movie theater. Everyone behaved during the movie because it was a special event.

Although the children had everything provided for their security and protection, they lacked the freedom to leave the village. Why? Because of concern for their safety. The sisters loved the children but could not give the love of a true mother and father. There were other needs that could not be provided by the village. Soon the children learned and understood that in life there is an abundance of joy, *happiness, and success; however, at times there might be hardships and problems. They had to discipline themselves and accept deficiencies and become courageous when hardships befell them.*

In time, the children had to leave the confines of the village and face life on their own. Were they ready to be independent? It is a pleasure to present to you the grown-up children of the children's village. YOU are the grown-up children. Congratulations for making a success of your lives. When I look at you today, I see fine men and women, contributing to the betterment of society. May God continue to bless and protect you and those dear to you on the path of your future undertakings. Be courageous, love God and neighbor, be happy, and remain loyal to your faith.

Looking around the room during the applause for Sister Angelita, I noted numerous alumni wiping tears from their faces. I think all of us felt something special from her rendition of "The Children's Village," our home, St. Hedwig Orphanage.

After the speeches were over and the luncheon was officially ended, those in attendance broke into smaller groups and began "visiting." But it did not end there. One or two from one group would approach another group and then another and another. It was rather neat to see these people really enjoying the moment. I cannot remember how many people approached me and thanked me for the "trip down memory lane." One man even asked me for a copy of my notes. That was when I found out that there would be no walking tour of the grounds of St. Hedwig Orphanage. Half of the buildings were already demolished, and the entire construction site was cordoned off with chain-linked fence. No Unauthorized Personnel signs were posted every thirty feet or so. I was truly disappointed.

THE BRICK

Someone had mentioned that they wanted a souvenir brick from the old "home." This triggered an idea among our group; and before you knew it, someone was going to see about getting a load of bricks from the construction site, clean them up, put a marker on them, and sell them to the St. Hedwig Alumni.

Rose Killips, her husband Don, and her granddaughter Jennifer tackled the task of having the bricks delivered to their home, cleaning the mortar off, affixing the memento tag, packaging and wrapping the bricks to be "post office ready." It took many months and a lot of hard work, but they were able to finish the job. I personally received my brick about a year after the luncheon. When I received my brick, it inspired me to write the following essay.

I received a package in the mail and knew immediately that it was my brick from St. Hedwig Orphanage. When I took the wrapping off and examined the brick's texture and attractive memorial marker, certain feelings coursed through my body and ended up in the pit of my stomach. For the longest time, I could not identify that particular feeling. Then it hit me: loss. The loss of a beginning or start. The loss of an identifiable place in my life that was very significant.

Just think about it. St. Hedwig is no more. Sure, there are photos and writings stored in the Historical Society for reference by our grandchildren, but the physical buildings, which the world knew as St. Hedwig Orphanage, are no longer a physical entity. It is merely a memory in our minds. Merely? Oh yes, what a memory. And not just for me. Just imagine all the children who walked the hallowed halls at one time or another from 1911 to 1961. All those individual memories. Good memories and bad memories. And everything in between.

Paczki Day, Punczki, Fat Covered Up, Visiting Sunday, the Friday-night movies, recess, dinnertime, scoldings by the mother superior, adoption interviews, dentist and doctor visits, oatmeal and raisins, and ginger cookies. And there was field day in the gym, basketball games against other schools, musicals and operettas put on by our own local talent, processions, and Camp Villa Marie. And don't forget the bus ride to the Pickwick Theater in Park Ridge to see a special showing of Gone with the Wind. *Then there was kitchen duty: peeling potatoes and scrubbing those monstrous pots and pans in the main kitchen. Yes, there were some spankings. Father Elmer's "persuader." Father Ed's Camel cigarettes. Monsignor Rusch's Perfecto Garcia Cigars. And his black Buick. It did not matter what year it was; it was always a black Buick. And vespers. Mass every day and at least twice on Sunday. Evening devotions. The duck pond. Let's not forget the shoe shop. And the mangle in the laundry. Big Emily, Bernice, Farmer Joe, Sister Edith, Jeep, Dr. Rosa, Mary Schwartz, the Stopka twins, the Biel brothers, Sister Marcy, Russ Lukes, Ronald Weiss. And who could forget Karen Wadas.*

I wonder where my brick came from. Was it the printery, where I spent many hours learning a trade that I never used? Maybe the infirmary where many of us spent time when we were sick. It could be that my particular brick came from the boy's side dorms or even the library. Maybe it came from the laundry or the chapel or the workers' quarters or even the gymnasium.

It matters not where my brick came from because it sits on my fireplace mantel in a place of honor. When I look at the brick, it may remind me of an incident that occurred so many years ago in a particular building that once was part of St. Hedwig Orphanage. St. Hedwig, you did good. I will certainly miss you, but the memories will always be there for me.

SISTER MARCY

The stories I have compiled about my experiences at St. Hedwig Orphanage would not be complete without a proper recognition of Sister Mary (Marcia) Marcy Baldys. If I had to pick one person in my life that had the most influence over me, I would have to select Sister Marcy. I have known and associated with many other nuns during my longer-than-eight-year stay at the orphanage. My involvement with Sister Marcy was brief. Nevertheless, the lone year that we interacted with each other made me the man I am today.

She taught me what hard work really was, but she helped me realize the results of my hard work and how rewarding it could be. Fairness was another of the special qualities that she instilled in me. It really helped me in my lengthy career in the Los Angeles Police Department. Marcy was not a women's libber, but she taught me to respect women, all women. She said I could never go wrong if I treated a woman as my equal. This attitude, which she helped bestow upon me, helped change my attitude toward women in police fieldwork. Up until then, I had always adhered to the belief that a woman should not be allowed to work the field as a police officer. Suddenly, my supervisors directed me to help change the attitudes of my subordinates. It was easy for me, thanks to Sister Marcy, to change my thinking. Ultimately, I became an ardent supporter of women officers.

At a gathering of the St. Hedwig Alumni Association in October 1996 at the White Eagle Restaurant, Niles, Illinois, I finally got to publicly thank Sister Marcy for guiding me through some pretty horrendous times. She was wise beyond her years when she dealt with the likes of Russ Lukes and me. She turned two of the biggest troublemakers into two very productive and successful citizens of our society. Please bear with me while I tell you a little bit about one of the finest teachers I have ever known.

Mary Baldys was born to Genevieve and Philip Baldys in West Hammond, Illinois, on March 23, 1915. She was baptized in the Catholic Church by the Reverend B. Nawakowski at St. Andrew the Apostle Church in Calumet City, Illinois, on April 4, 1915. She attended elementary school in Medford, Wisconsin, where her parents moved to when she was four years of age. She graduated from elementary school in May 1929.

After a year as a freshman at Medford High School, Mary entered the aspirancy at Good Counsel High School, Chicago, Illinois, on August 27, 1929. She graduated from Good Counsel in June 1933 and, days later, entered the postulancy of the Felician Sisters at the Mother of Good Counsel Province. A year later, in August 1934, she was initiated into the life of a Felician sister.

On August 23, 1935, Sister Mary Marcy made her first profession of annual vows until she pronounced her final vows on August 23, 1941.One of her first teaching assignments came in 1933 at St. John of God Parish in Chicago, Illinois. She taught the fifth grade for about one year.

In 1935, she transferred to St. Joseph Parish in Chicago as a fifth-grade teacher. She remained in this assignment for five years. In 1940, Sister Marcy was sent to Birmingham, Alabama, teaching African Americans at the Holy Family Mission School in Ensley. She remained in this assignment for approximately six years.

Her first stint at St. Hedwig Orphanage, also known as St. Hedwig Industrial School, in Chicago, Illinois, came in 1946 as a seventh-grade teacher. After approximately three years, she left for an assignment at St. Bruno's Parish in Chicago, teaching the eighth grade. The following year, she was assigned to St. Hyacinth Parish in La Salle, Illinois, teaching the eighth grade. She remained at St. Hyacinth for about five years. From there, she went to Holy Rosary Parish in North Chicago, Illinois, for a two-year tour of duty.

In 1955, Sister Marcy returned to St. Hedwig Orphanage as a high school teacher. She remained there until sometime in 1960. From 1960 to 1961, Sister Marcy taught the eighth grade at St. Turibius Parish in Chicago. From 1961 to 1963, she left for assignment in Brazil. She was commissioned to set up a library for the American embassy students at Our Lady of Mercy High School in Rio de Janeiro, Brazil. The library was to be affiliated with the Catholic University of America and accredited by the United States Southern Association.

She returned from Brazil in 1963 and took a position at Holy Innocents Parish, teaching the eighth grade for one year. The following year, she taught the sixth grade. She transferred to St. Helen Parish in Chicago where she taught the eighth grade. A year later, she was transferred to Saints Peter and Paul Parish, Chicago, where she taught grades 7 and 8 over a two-year period.

She taught seventh grade at Good Shepherd Parish, Chicago, in 1968. In 1969, she returned to St. Bruno Parish as the eighth-grade teacher and, in 1970, as the high school librarian at St. Joseph Parish. In 1971, she took on the position of librarian and religion teacher at Our Lady of Ransom Parish in Niles, Illinois. She was assigned to St. Florian Parish in Hatley, Wisconsin, where she taught grades 4 and 5 in 1972. She also served as the librarian for the school.

In 1973, Sister Marcy transferred to St. Stanislaus Bishop and Martyr Parish in Posen, Illinois. She taught the sixth grade and served as the school librarian for six years. In 1978, she was assigned to St. Francis Hospital in Milwaukee, Wisconsin, as a pastoral associate. The following year, she went to Kansas City, Missouri, as a student in the CPE program. In 1980 to 1982, she returned to the provincial house, Chicago, Illinois, at the Felician College as a teacher and associate librarian. She spent the next four years at St. Mary's Hospital in Centralia, Illinois, as a pastoral associate. Finally in 1985, she was assigned to Our Lady of Good Counsel Infirmary, Chicago, Illinois, in the pastoral ministry.

Somehow, this lady found the time to get her master's degree in library science from Rosary College in River Forest, Illinois, in 1961. She also managed to become an accomplished and published poet. Sister Marcy's poetry can be viewed at the following two Web sites:

http://www.poetry.com/poets/SisterMMarcyBaldys.html
http://www.poetry.com/poets/SisterM.MarcyBaldys.html

As you can see, this has been one very busy Felician sister. She had been involved in religious life for sixty-six years. At the time of her death on November 22, 1999, she had allowed us to be associated with her for eighty-four years of life.

I know that she is in a better place and in a position of influence. I hope and pray that Sister Marcy will put in a good word for me if she thinks that I deserve it. May she rest in peace. She certainly deserves her place in heaven. I give her all the credit for keeping me out of Joliet State Penitentiary. You taught me well, Sister.

EPILOGUE

Thousands of children lived in St. Hedwig Orphanage during the years 1911 to 1961. It would be difficult to come up with an accurate figure. Though orphanages are not in "vogue" during these modern times, it makes one wonder about our present methods of dealing with dysfunctional families. Whether it be from death, divorce, or even political reasons, there has got to be a better method of taking care of the thousands of children caught up in some challenging circumstances. Spending one's formative years in an orphanage, although not ideal, wasn't all that bad. I believe it made a good person out of me. But that was only because of certain individual efforts by some of the nuns who participated in my life during those years. Under the current laws of the land, some of those involved in my upbringing could possibly be brought up on abuse charges if those incidents occurred today.

Many of the alumni of St. Hedwig Orphanage may not be setting the world on fire with their various successes. They may not dress in Gucci clothes or drive the most expensive cars. However, they are good people, well mannered, who know right from wrong. Their experiences as children may not have been ideal, but somewhere along the road, they learned invaluable lessons from the sisters at St. Hedwig. Of course, the priests backed up the sisters with some force when necessary.

Monsignor Francis Rusch, the headmaster of St. Hedwig for so many years, set the course so long ago. This disciplinarian did not know the meaning of the word "fail." He loved children and wanted the best for his wards. Even when you were in trouble, you could sense the love that was in this man's heart. Some people may feel that the orphanage concept may not work in this day and age, but during my personal era, it was the best there ever was.

CPSIA information can be obtained at www.ICGtesting.com
Printed in the USA
BVOW011904280113

311790BV00002B/102/P